BOOK OF SUCCESSFUL BATHROOMS

Chin-deep soaking, Oriental style, provides luxury element in this compartmented bathroom. Shoji screen slides to close off water closet area, while total room design highlights the warm wood and uncluttered lines of decorative plastic laminates. Photo by Kohler Co.

Today's Early American look can be practical as well as attractive. This remodeled bath has textured Marlite paneling in wormy chestnut pattern, durable plastic laminate countertop and self-rimming lavatory bowls.

Garden bath with raised platform provides area for relaxing on foam cushions as well as an area for morning exercises. Photo by Universal-Rundle.

Dressing room baths are part of many master suites, providing luxurious comfort and privacy. Armstrong Fancy Free flooring, fabrics, and vinyl wallcovering have been coordinated for this setting.

This spacious tub and shower area opens onto its own sun terrace through sliding glass doors. For showering, the entire room becomes the stall shower with a high shower head for "him" and a lower one for "her." The ceramic mosaic tile used for the floor and walls harmonizes with the blue of the Eljer sunken tub. A luminous ceiling provides ample illumination.

Old brick Masonite panels provide a bright treatment for a small bathroom. Note the space-saving corner lavatory basin. Folding, flexible shower door at right adds greater feeling of openness to the room.

Leaded glass window and clearstory ceiling above the bath add to the illumination of this bathroom. The tub appears partially sunken though the addition of a step. Floor-to-ceiling linen cabinet and twin-bowl vanity are surfaced with Formica plastic laminate.

BOOK OF
Successful
Bathrooms

by Joseph F. Schram

STRUCTURES PUBLISHING COMPANY
Farmington, Michigan   1976

Copyright © 1976 Structures Publishing Co.
Farmington, Michigan

Manufactured in the United States of America

Book designed by Richard Kinney

Book edited by Shirley M. Horowitz

Current Printing (last digit)
10 9 8 7 6 5 4 3 2 1

International Standard Book Number: 0–912336–16–1 (hardcover)
0–912336–17–X (paper)

Library of Congress Catalog Card Number: LC 75–31489

Structures Publishing Co.
Box 423, Farmington, Mich. 48024

Library of Congress Cataloging in Publication Data

Schram, Joseph F
   Book of successful bathrooms.

   (Successful books)
   Includes index.
   1. Bathrooms. I. Title. II. Title: Successful
bathrooms.
TH6485.S38   643'.52   75-31489
ISBN 0-912336-16-1
ISBN 0-912336-17-X pbk.

CONTENTS

1905663

FOREWORD

Less than a quarter-century ago the bathroom was the most neglected area of the house. Today it receives as much attention as any other living area and is often adapted to reflect the taste of the owner and family lifestyle.

In recent years designers and builders of new homes have introduced a new opulence to the bathroom as a means of attracting more buyers. The bathroom has been increased in size; color has become a dominant factor in the selection of fixtures, surfaces, and accessories; and decorative items once found only in the family room are now common to the bathroom—reading materials, small art pieces, exercise facilities, lamps, and carpets.

Homeowners, following the lead of designers and builders, are now remodeling their bathrooms at the rate of 2.5 million per year, accounting for a sizeable share of the $30 billion spent annually on residential remodeling programs.

The thoughtful design and remodeling of bathrooms involve usage of modern fixtures taking up less space than previous ones; fixtures which provide more than one function, such as the combination tub-shower or lavatory-grooming center; materials that need no periodic refinishing; and attractively coordinated accessories. A bathroom can cost up to $10,000 or more, yet many improvements can be incorporated into an existing bathroom on a budget that is well within the average family means. Truly, the bathroom is one area of the home where individuality can be accomplished through imagination.

The trend today is to larger bathrooms which afford the user a place to relax and to escape daily cares. Many new bathrooms have become multi-purpose rooms complete with exercise equipment, sun lamps, loungers, etc. Often the setting opens onto a private patio, garden, or sun deck. Some bathrooms include or are adjacent to a sauna bath or built-in steam bath. And still others, site permitting, provide a floor-to-ceiling view of the surrounding area. The bath itself can be circular, slanted, or sunken.

We are pleased to add *Successful Bathrooms* to our successful series of home improvement books and believe that you, the reader, will find in this book most helpful and specific information to guide you in improving your bathroom. Our author has been writing on this subject for over 25 years, reporting nationally on the thousands of new bathroom products, styles and concepts brought forth by builders, researchers, and designers.

We encourage you to make use of these products, materials and ideas . . . to create your own SUCCESSFUL BATHROOMS.

R. J. Lytle, Publisher
Structures Publishing Company

This photo from an early 20th Century architectural book explains that "the bathroom has become a permanent part of the well-to-do English household . . . with expensive fittings placed at dignified distances from one another . . . and central space ample enough for moving freely about, even exercising."

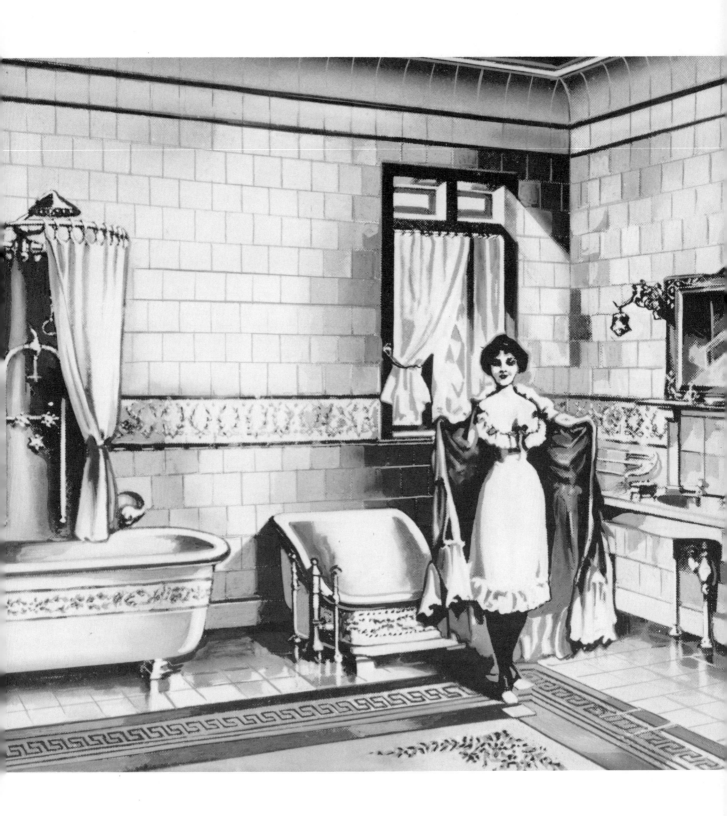

INTRODUCTION

The first "bathroom" was neither a bath nor a room . . . it was the river bank of prehistoric days!

The first recorded bathroom site was built over 4000 years ago in a palace called the Labyrinth (that same Labyrinth known as the home of the Minotaur), in the Cretan city of Cnossos. Designed for the king, it was connected to the throne room. Crete became, in many ways, the source for later Greek practices.

The ancient Greek tradition of taking cold showers by pouring water over oneself ultimately evolved into the public bath system, a friendly routine that the Romans further developed into public swimming pools. That bathing occupied an important place in the life of the Greeks is indicated by vase paintings which depict baths and showers—elaborate scenes suggesting that bathing had become an accepted and valued activity. The splendid palaces of the Aegean civilization provide the earliest well-preserved examples of private bathrooms. These rooms, called "loutron," followed the early patterns set forth by Cnossus and Phaistos.

Around 52 A.D. an Emperor seeking political support built a new public bath as a popularity gimmick. It was an ornate establishment decorated with priceless marbles, columns and statues, mosaics for the pavements, and major works of art adorning the walls. The fall of the Roman Empire brought a decline in bathing until the Middle Ages when, during the 11th century, the wealthy put wooden tubs in their chambers. Private bathrooms were reserved for the rich for many years to come. A measure of the prestige accorded the bath can be gathered from the statement once put forth by one of Queen Elizabeth's ministers to the effect that "the Queen taketh a bath *every month,* whether she needeth it or no." Marble, stained glass, and other expensive materials marked the Byzantine or Moorish baths of the mid-1800's. The Germans later developed corrugated iron bath houses in which showers were used.

The American Indians were the first inhabitants on this continent to employ a bathroom. In actuality these were "sweat lodges" in which the Indians steamed themselves, communal fashion. The lodges were constructed of bark, branches, and hardened mud. The world's modern bathroom styles, as we know them, were developed in England. They were unequalled for luxury up until 1910, being private, large, and fully furnished. The first bathtub was installed in the United States in the early part of this century, reportedly in Cincinnati. This move brought about the demise of the wooden or metal tub set next to the wood-fired kitchen stove, and heralded greater privacy, convenience, luxury, and comfort.

Drastic changes have since occurred in bathroom styles. Those of the early 1900's compare to today's bath just as the Model-T does to the Lincoln Continental. And more changes are to be expected as will be seen in this *Book of Successful Bathrooms.* With new tastes and technologies will come new models of the "ideal bathroom," but whatever new ideas emerge the best bathroom will always be the one that responds to your individual needs. So draw the water, sit back, and see what you've been missing . . . what you could be planning for that new home or remodeling program.

Formica plastic laminates in floral and woodgrain patterns create the decor of this bathroom, with gold countertop, carpet and fixtures providing the color. Seven mirrors are part of the wall decoration.

Walls, ceiling, and cabinetry of this masculine bath for a modern A-frame home are U.S. Plywood Roughtex. The countertops and floor are American Olean ceramic tile in an unglazed, earthy hearth shade. Wainscoting and tub surround are Redi-Set 300, sheets of pregrouted ceramic tile in a warm autumn gold glaze. The fixtures are Kohler and accessories are North and South American Indian crafts.

Provincial bathroom settings are accomplished with white and gold vanity cabinets and matching linen units. Twin mirrors and open, carpeted area allow easy use by two persons. Nutone photo by Marian Finney.

The bather in this oval custom tub-shower, in Sunset Orange Caribbean ceramic tile by American Olean, can look out into a private Japanese garden. Inlet valves are for creating whirlpool action. The flexible shower arm allows localized use. Sliding glass doors open onto the garden deck.

Mural, planks, and prefinished wall panels of this eye-catching bathroom are Marlite for easy maintenance with a damp cloth. Countertop surfaces are plastic laminate, again for easy cleaning.

Japanese architecture continues to influence bathroom design in the United States. This serene room has the pure textures of bamboo, quarry tile, and natural woods. The tub wall and countertop are covered with laminated plastic in a glossy marble pattern. Fixtures in the 11 × 13 room are by Kohler.

Rustic charm has been captured and combined with
contemporary convenience in this Kohler bathroom. The
random plank floor and rough plaster walls provide a cozy
setting for cherished possessions. The bath vanity with
plastic laminate countertop is by Connor. The room is 10
feet wide, 11 1/2 feet deep.

Gerber decorator lavatory bowls are vitreous china units
with lifetime patterns in black or gold. Both self-rimming
and under-counter types are offered.

Separate shower and tub add to the functional aspect of this bathroom featuring Formica's 202 Panel System. A luminous ceiling is framed in same material as mirrors.

Decorative hardware by Ajax and colorful knick knacks enhance this Early American compartmented bath. Cabinets are natural wood with plastic laminate countertop matching color of the bathtub.

Masculinity is the key note for this "his" area, which includes a six-foot wardrobe closet with folding doors, built-in drawers, toiletry case, lavatory and cushioned seat. The entire area can be closed off from the balance of the bathroom, which also includes a similar-size "her" area. All of the cabinetwork is finished in Formica and the plumbing fixtures are by Eljer.

Lavatory faucets are now available in popular decorator colors as well as chrome and goldplate. Mansfield's Waverly 4-inch centerset model has a squared-off look with no angles or crevices to collect dirt.

No special care is required for cleaning decorated china lavatory bowls by Briggs. The units come in four lavatory styles, nine designs and six colors.

Bright wall and cabinet is in contrast to white countertop and Ajax decorative hardware, plu white bathroom fixtures.

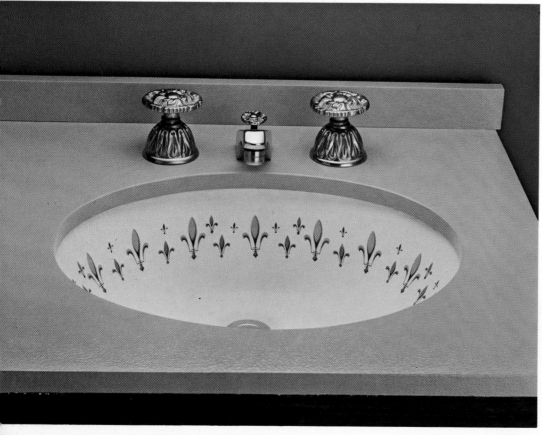

Plastic laminate and drop-in self-rimming lavatory from Universal-Rundle create easy-to-clean arrangement.

Low-silhouette design of this siphon-jet toilet by Borg-Warner Plumbing Products can be attributed to Cycolac ABS, a durable, hard thermoplastic which allows thinner reservoir walls. The unit weighs only 9 pounds, yet holds the same amount of water as vitreous china models.

A built-in tile bench above the radiant heating unit doubles as a bench for basking under sunlamps or a bench for potted plants. The floor is random-set green slate by American Olean. (two views)

1 Planning and Remodeling Your Bathroom

Planning a new bathroom or remodeling an existing one begins with a determination of the desired floor plan. Often this decision will be made for you for the most part by the amount of space available, but if you are beginning from "scratch," you will find a wide latitude in what you can plan and obtain.

In planning a bathroom for a new home or in adding a complete new bathroom to an existing dwelling, it is good to begin by asking yourself a number of questions. The answers will provide you, and those assisting you in the project, with necessary facts and objectives to be incorporated into the overall plan. The most important questions to be considered are:

- What area of the home will be served by this bathroom?
- Who will be the principal users of the bathroom—Parents? Children? Guests?
- Will this bathroom be an integral part of the master suite, or should it be "family" in nature to serve several bedrooms adjacent to its location?
- How much space can be allotted to the new bathroom?
- What is the "outside" cost figure that can be considered?
- What basic fixtures are "musts" in the new room? Tub or shower?
- How much space should be planned for bathroom storage?

- Will the room be used for other than normal bathroom purposes—will it also serve as an exercise room, an added place to relax, or an extension of the master suite?

In this section of *Successful Bathrooms* you will find photographs and floor plans of bathroom designs which have been used in many recently constructed and remodeled homes throughout the country. These plans have been carefully thought out with regard to fixture placement, necessary storage, movement within the room, possible use by more than one person at a time, location of doors and windows and other design factors.

The Master Suite Bath

Builders, architects and decorators have found the incorporation of a tasteful master bedroom-bathroom suite to be a key factor in attracting new home sales. This is especially true when the price of the home is $50,000 or more, and when the buyer has already owned a "tract" home with a cramped minimum three-fixture bathroom that has caused problems morning after morning for several years.

Today's master suite may be viewed as a private living area for the "master" and "mistress" of the home.

Silver and white predominate in this master bathroom with foil-covered walls and raised bathing-relaxing platform. The off-the-floor built-in vanity is finished in square-edged decorative plastic laminate. Glass shelves show off a collection of bibelots. Universal-Rundle photo.

It is often equipped with an easy chair for the man of the house, a lounge for the wife, a stereo, a television, or other "specialties" geared to individual or combined interests. Personal preference is the key to the design of this type of bedroom-bathroom area. Attention, however, should be given to including:

- Single or double lavatory bowls in easy-to-maintain countertops with cabinets which provide ample storage area for common bathroom items such as towels, cosmetics, tissue, etc.

- Ample storage area for his and her clothes, shoes and accessories. You'll note the dressing room approach in many of the accompanying floor plans. The tub or shower and toilet have been "compartmentalized" away from the dressing area, which includes the wash basin and vanity.
- Separate or combination bathtub-shower units to maintain the flexibility of the bathroom, both now and in the event of a future sale of the dwelling. All showers and no bathtub will be a drawback when reselling the home.

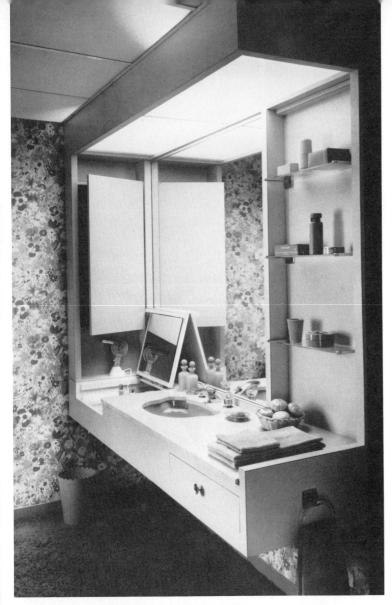

The "her" area of a master bathroom suite in this home features a vanity counter with special features—a jewelry drawer, concealed storage, glass shelves for perfumes, and a mirrored make-up compartment illuminated from below. Photo by Eljer.

It's just a matter of steps between this master bathroom and bedroom. To emphasize the modern decor, a large vanity was included on the main wall, which also features a gold-crafted Marlite mural panel. Other plastic-finished paneling surfaces the remainder of wall area and the ceiling is a wall-to-wall luminous grid system.

Real semi-precious stones have been used in the fittings of this Sherle Wagner bathroom. Rose quartz combines with 24-carat goldplate. The muted pink tone is repeated in a palest, delicate shade of rose aurora onyx and marble in the hand-carved marble bath, with fluted pedestals built in at each end. The same shell motif was used for the hand-carved wash basin.

Singing star Dionne Warwick's bathroom has sheet mirror on the door surfaces of walk-in closets and a sunken Sherle Wagner bathtub. The indoor-outdoor Hollywood bath is fully carpeted and includes theatrical-style lighting.

White stucco walls, shutters and rich dark beams were used to create this Mediterranean bathroom by American-Standard. The fixtures are green, as is the tile floor.

Compartmented water closet area of this bathroom can be closed off via folding panel doors surfaced in the same vinyl material as surrounding walls. American-Standard photo.

The Compartmented Bathroom

Compartmented bathrooms which can serve two or more persons at the same time increase the room's efficiency, often require little more floor space than an open floor plan. New and remodeled bathrooms can be divided into compartments by installing hinged or sliding doors, screens, or partitions. The basic compartmented bath separates the lavatory from the tub and water closet to allow two people simultaneous use of the room. More elaborate bathrooms offer twin-basin lavatories, one or two separate water closets, and a tub or shower in still another section of the room.

Your choice of compartmented bathrooms will depend upon the number of persons who may need to use it at the same time, and the floor space available. Care should be taken that swinging doors do not inconvenience those using the room.

A compartmented water closet area enables dual use of this bathroom, equipped with twin self-rimming lavatories. Full-length mirror is mounted on clothes closet at left. Window treatment above water closet is repeated in tub area. Kohler photo.

A sliding pocket door converts this master bath into two separated, private areas. Louvered doors, stained to match the Marlite Barnside paneling on the walls, conceal his-'n-her medicine cabinets on each side of the mirror. The soffit houses fluorescent fixtures illuminating the vanity area. Standard window shutters—mounted on a shower track with louvers slanted inward—add to the rugged appearance supplied by the paneling.

The Garden Bathroom

The impact of California home design on building styles in recent years has resulted in national acceptance of and desire for the garden bathroom—affording the user a garden view, a private patio, or a combination of both.

The glass wall or sliding glass door which opens onto a private garden or patio gives the room a larger, more luxurious aspect. Tempered glass is recommended, and in many areas required, by the local building code. Glass areas needn't be confined to walls free of plumbing fixtures. Delightful settings can be obtained by placing viewing windows above built-in vanities and adjacent to sunken or raised tubs or tub-shower combinations. If the bath garden is entirely secluded, the scene can be enhanced with outdoor lighting, thus keeping the large expanse of glass from appearing black and cold at night. Draw draperies can be installed in the bathroom across a garden glass wall for night privacy, if the drapes are not close to the shower.

Screens, fences, and plantings furnish the privacy necessary to a garden bathroom. The garden itself may be large enough for sunbathing and relaxation or it may be so small as to offer a view of only a few selected plantings from the bathroom proper. Access to the garden area can be provided via a gate in the garden fence, avoiding the need to carry garden supplies through the home. This arrangement simplifies plant watering and minimizes dirt tracked into the bathroom.

Some garden bathrooms offer the option of indoor or outdoor showering by including a second shower on the outside bath wall. This can be especially convenient when the garden is near a swimming pool, so that swimmers can shower without entering the bathroom itself.

Plantings in the patio, bathroom or garden should be selected for their decorative appeal and their ability to grow in confined space. Most house plants thrive in the warm, humid atmosphere of a bathroom. Some of the most successful are: Orchids, Chinese evergreen, African violets, Philodendron, Grape ivy, and Fittonia. But flowers and shrubs to be used in outside gardens should be chosen with climate in mind in order to avoid bare grey branches in the winter or parched, wilted leaves in the summer. Care must be taken to place plants so they receive ample sunlight (or a proper artificial substitute), and so that shower water does not strike them, bruising the foliage or causing rot.

A variety of decorating ideas went into creating this garden
bathroom—wall shelves for plants; mirror squares; a plastic
skylight; and decorative plastic laminate countertop with
"his" and "her" self-rimming bowls by Gerber Plumbing
Fixtures Corp.

Fixed tempered glass along the back and one end of the
bathtub afford the bather a private garden view. The
stretch-out Kohler tub is six feet long and three feet wide
with gently sloping back for reclining ease.

Evocative of the Orient, this bath has sliding glass shoji screens enclosing the shower stall and serving as a passageway from the vanity to the tub area, which is decorated as an indoor Japanese garden. The sunken tub is lined with 2 × 2 unglazed American Olean ceramic mosaics. The twin-bowl vanity with center dressing table is topped with plastic laminate.

The Powder Room or Lavatory

Half-baths, better known as the powder room or lavatory, have become extremely handy in homes of all sizes. These rooms can be located in areas convenient to the "living area" of a home, i.e., the kitchen, den and family room. The powder room eliminates the bathtub while providing the other major bathroom fixtures, namely the water closet and lavatory basin. If the primary users are to be children, this room can be designed for minimum maintenance. It can be more formally decorated if it will serve adults and guests.

Because you won't have to contend with the water vapor problem created by a tub or shower you can use decorative objects in a powder room that would not be practical in a family bath. Chain lamps, picture-frame mirrors, and cabinets contribute to a pleasant setting while at the same time giving an impression of spaciousness. Skylights are often used in powder rooms to provide natural illumination, especially in rooms without windows. Combination light fixture-exhaust fans are also popular.

As shown in the accompanying floor plans, care should be taken that the door swings toward a clear wall space whenever possible and not against the water closet or lavatory.

1905663

Use of corner area for lavatory installation leaves room for a sit-down area in this powder room, as well as storage space below the basin. Plastic-finished Marlite planks were used for the walls, gold and black marble pattern for the countertop.

Art objects need not be confined to the living and dining rooms. Both built-in and free-standing display units add to this bathroom setting by American-Standard.

The Special Bathroom

Special considerations should be made in planning a bathroom intended for children, for a retirement home, for a vacation home, or for an invalid or handicapped person.

Children's Baths

The children's bath should be a room that is easily cleaned. Surfaces should withstand splashing, spotting, and dripping; tile is therefore more practical than carpeting.

The children's bath should be readily accessible from children's bedrooms. Door locks should be the type that can be opened from outside the bathroom if necessary. A door to the outside is a convenience when using the bathroom as a "mud" or "cleaning up" room on rainy days.

Manufacturers recommend using standard-size fixtures for the children's bathroom, along with built-in steps or stools to bring the wash basin within reach of a child's shorter arms. Wash basins can be installed at a lower height, but as the children grow the installation

would be uncomfortable and would have to be replaced. Single-handle faucets are simpler and safer than separate hot and cold water controls which require mixing the water to the desired temperature. Showers can include two shower heads—the top one plugged initially with the lower one operative for youngsters. As the children grow, the lower one can be plugged and the upper one put into use. Electrical plans for this type of bathroom should include a built-in night light; all forms of ceiling fans and heaters should be operated by a timer control which will shut the units off if the children forget to do so.

If the water closet stall is equipped with a door, the door should swing outward and be a minimum of 32 inches wide to accommodate a wheelchair. Minimum depth of the stall should be 60 inches, and the total width should be at least 36 inches to allow for heavy-duty 4-foot-long grab-safety bars on each side of the toilet. The walls may enclose the area from floor to ceiling (see attached drawing), or partial-height walls can flank the water closet.

As noted in the accompanying sketches, floor- or wall-mounted toilet bowls should be 18 inches in height

Planned to answer children's needs from infancy through the teens, this bathroom has a wide countertop alongside the deep lavatory. The bottom drawer pulls out to become a step and can be easily converted to conventional drawer space at a later time. Recessed shelf above towels accommodates plastic glasses. Folding door and companion lavatory on one side of the wall, second lavatory and bath on other side, prevent tie-ups as children mature.

from rim to floor and the front edge should be no more than 29-3/4 inches from the wall. Grab bars are centered on the front edge of the bowl to give two feet of bar area in front of and two feet along side of the bowl.

Lavatory installations with special fixtures for easy access to a wheelchair patient are available. Some models have curved front rims for additional comfort and convenience. The rim-to-floor measurement should be 34 inches and fittings should be equipped with 4-inch wrist controls. Standard lavatory size for this type of installation is a 20-inch width and a 27-inch depth. A concealed arm support is required for the fixture.

Shower stalls for the physically handicapped should be 36 inches wide and 36 inches deep, and be equipped with an L-shaped heavy-duty grab bar (see sketch). All fittings should be placed within easy reach of the user. Recommended installation heights for Kohler fittings are detailed in sketches. A folding seat, if used, must be raised or lowered without difficulty.

Bathtubs with grip rails securely built into the tub walls are recommended. The tub models available can be recessed between three walls or, for models which have no apron, may be installed as a peninsula in the room. Slip-free bottoms are a must, preferably a ridged surface rather than a mat which could slide when wet.

This children's bath has a resilient floor surface, vinyl wall covering, plastic laminate tub surround, and lavatory countertop for easy clean-up. The corner tub has a slip-resistant bottom. Shelves on ladder are removable for easy placement at desired heights. Other rungs serve as towel racks. American-Standard photo.

Kohler's Highline toilet for use by senior citizens and handicapped persons has extra height—18 inches from floor to the top of the rim. The siphon jet unit has an elongated bowl, large water area, and large passageway. The fixture comes in white and in a variety of colors.

Features for the Elderly or the Handicapped

For the Elderly

Bathrooms designed for retirement homes should stress safety, convenience, and easy maintenance. Walls, floors, and accessories should be constructed to eliminate the need for periodic refinishing; plastic laminates, ceramic tile, and plastic-coated hardboard are the most popular and effective materials for this type of bathroom.

In designing a new retirement bathroom, make the doorway wide enough to accommodate a wheelchair and select a lock style used by hospitals so that the door can be opened from the outside in an emergency. Door knobs as well as light switches should be 36" above floor level—lower knobs and switches require stooping, which might strain already painful muscles. Floors should be of a nonslip material, and if carpeting is used it should be taped to the floor. Scatter rugs are dangerous, and should be avoided. Bathtubs and shower stalls should include a built-in seat or ledge. Both installations should include sturdy grab bars at both sitting and standing height. Grab bars are also desirable on either side of the toilet, making it easier to rise. Extra-large medicine cabinets are recommended so that all medicines are clearly visible. Brighter illumination than usual from both natural and artificial sources adds a further degree of safety and convenience, as does an adequate night light. Single-handle lavatory and shower controls are easiest to operate. The installation of a pressure and temperature control valve in the shower prevents accidental blasts of hot or cold water.

For the Handicapped

The designing and adding of special bathroom features for a physically handicapped person requires the selection of special plumbing fixtures suited to the user's needs. The fixtures should provide maximum convenience for the patient or senior citizen, and ease of cleaning.

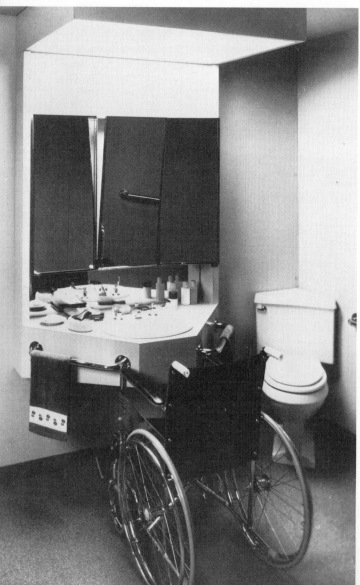

Planned to provide easy access for wheelchairs or crutches, this bathroom space designed for the handicapped person includes Eljer's 18-inch-high corner toilet. The lavatory drop-in bowl is fitted with wrist-action handles for easier use by an arthritic. The center mirror is adjustable for use when sitting down or standing up. Heavy-duty grab bars double as towel bars.

Widely used in private residences, hospitals, nursing homes, and rehabilitation centers, is this American-Standard Bath-Lift. The chair seat swings out for patient and returns easily to position in the tub. A fingertip adjustment lets the seat glide gently downward. When bathing is completed, chair ascends smoothly.

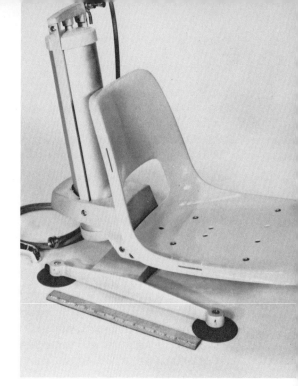

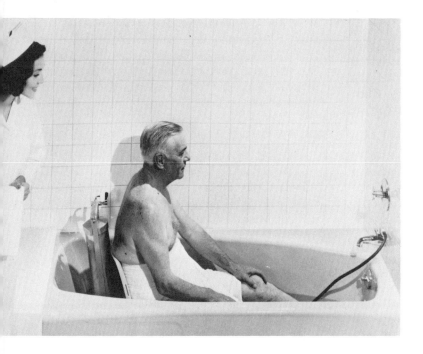

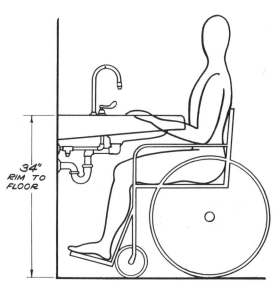

34"
RIM TO
FLOOR

The Morningside by Kohler has a curved front to accommodate wheelchair patients. The basin is shallow, offering leg room below. This fixture extends 27 inches from the wall to front edge and is only 20 inches wide. It can be equipped with wrist-control fittings.

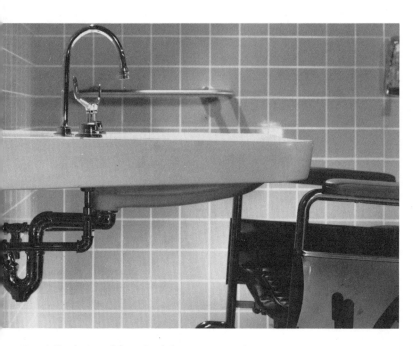

Specially designed for wheelchair patients, this American-Standard lavatory has a roll-under design which eliminates possible interference of the legs or chair with water supplies, pipe or lavatory. The fixture is available, with punching, on 12-inch centers for wrist handles or 4-inch centers for push-pull fittings.

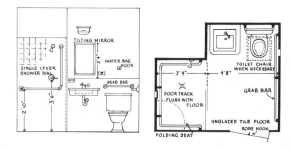

These sketches show suggested placement and dimensions for a bathroom to be used by a physically handicapped person.

Vacation Bath Plans

The vacation home bath generally is designed to be as compact and economical as possible, and to require minimum maintenance and upkeep. These requisites somewhat restrict the design as well as size.

In planning a vacation home bathroom, it is wise to check the sanitary code requirements in rural areas before settling on the plumbing layout. Often, requirements will differ from urban codes. Care should be given to planning a drainage system which can be easily drained and closed down for long periods of time when the vacation home is not in use, and which can be put into operation quickly at the opening of a vacation season.

Locating the bathroom "wet" wall on the back of the kitchen "wet" wall will save dollars. Likewise, selection of white fixtures will reduce costs. Use of a shower stall instead of a bathtub will save floor space, as will a sliding pocket door as opposed to a swing door. If a swimming pool is involved you may wish to also consider an exterior entry door to the bathroom. The use of a compartmented plan with a double set of lavatory bowls may be essential if you plan to have guests as well as family staying in the vacation home.

BATHROOM FLOOR PLANS

While the most economical plumbing arrangement incorporates all fixtures on a single wall, this greatly reduces the design and use acceptability of the room and is often thereby discarded in favor of using one or more additional "wet" walls.

The following floor plans for your new or remodeled bath should be reviewed keeping in mind that the ideas presented can be combined and expanded to suit your particular needs or tastes.

Master Bathrooms

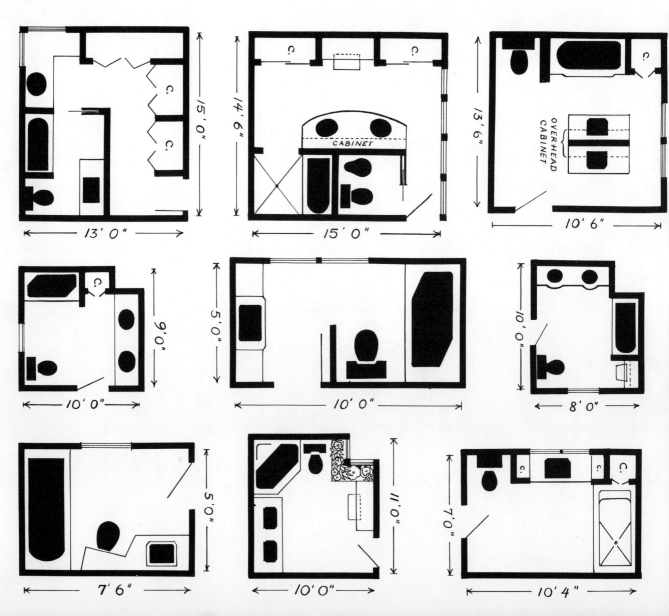

Compartmentalized Bathrooms

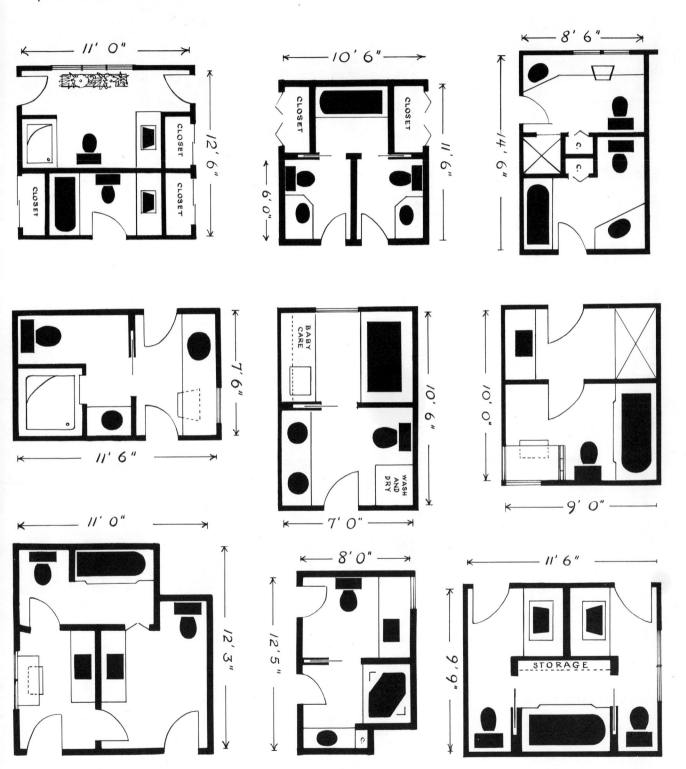

Garden Bathrooms

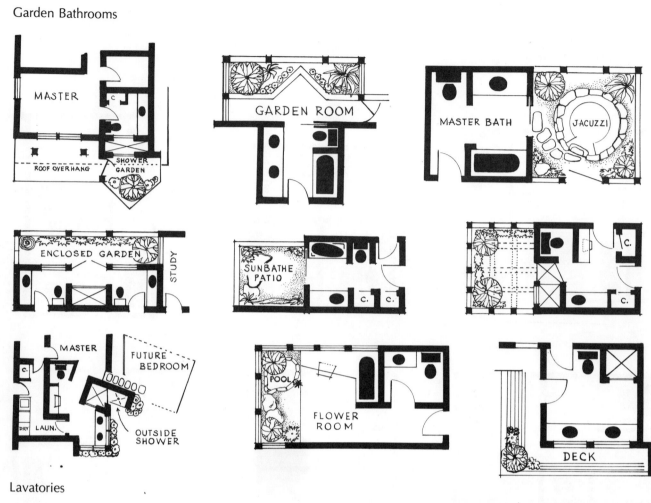

Lavatories

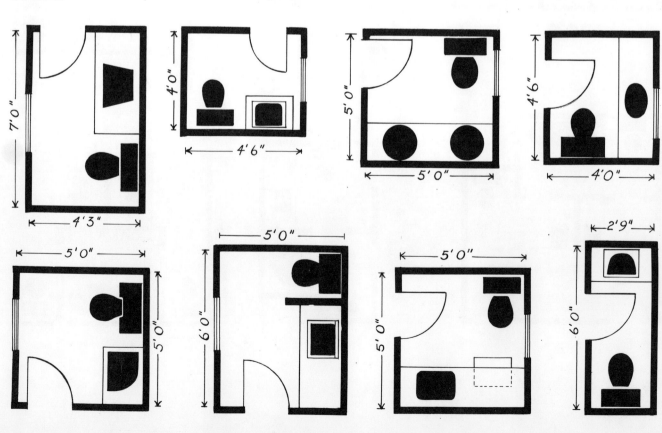

What Remodeling Can Accomplish

Bathroom remodeling can accomplish miracles as depicted here in the renewal of an 1880-vintage master bathroom in Philadelphia. The original fixtures were installed during World War I. The newest fixture was the pedestal lavatory; the water closet and bathtub were older.

A previous "remodeling" replaced the old hot-water radiator with a more modern under-the-window unit. The old corner medicine cabinet had been removed, but paint continued to peel and the floor tiles heaved as the tileboard bulged.

Using a modern layout in the same space, a tub was sunk into an unused back stairwell, and was supported by steel I-beams resting on iron braces bolted to the joists. Beyond the arch, the toilet was placed to one side, with a new linen closet occupying the other. Window size was reduced.

On the right side of the bathroom a long decorative plastic laminate countertop houses twin lavatories above added storage area. Vinyl wall covering and American Olean ceramic tile were used for the walls, with large 12-inch-square tiles for the floor.

2 Color in the Bathroom

Color and accessories are the decorator's prime allies in achieving a beautiful bathroom. Every item in the bath contributes to the total scheme and thus must be given attention and consideration in relation to the effect desired (see also the color section of this book).

Most manufacturers of bathroom fixtures offer both pastel and bright accent colors in addition to standard white units. Colors variation from firm to firm are seen not only in their enticing trade names (Expresso, Sunflower, Pink Champagne, etc.), but also in the color shading or intensity. As much as possible, therefore, you should select complete "sets" of fixtures from a single manufacturer in order to insure consistent color match. Bright and bold colors have taken over the bathroom in recent years, just as they have the kitchen and other rooms of the modern home. Rather than "relying on the towels" to provide the color, designers use the major elements (the fixtures) to set the scene, and then build around them for the finished setting.

The colors chosen for the fixtures determine to a large extent the decorative scheme for the floor, walls, ceiling, and accessories. Suppliers and designers recommend that you choose a wall color that harmonizes with the fixtures, rather than trying to match it exactly. Light colors tend to make bathrooms appear larger and brighter. They also aid in room illumination, making it easier to shave and apply make-up.

Because surfaces such as floors, countertops and walls (if they are surfaced with permanent plastic laminate or ceramic tile) must be considered at least semipermanent and are unlikely to be changed very often, they should complement the fixtures. Painted walls and those finished with flexible materials can be redecorated more easily, allowing a wider range of selection.

Carpeting has become acceptable and desirable in the bathroom. Generally, it should be the same color as that in the bedroom if the bathroom is part of a master suite or a combination dressing room-bath arrangement. Likewise, a bathroom opening off a hall should be compatible with the hall wall, floor and ceiling colors.

The color most often chosen for ceilings is white, as it reflects more light and plays a neutral role in the total color scheme. If wood or wood paneling is used for the ceiling, or if the ceiling is painted a dark color, plan to provide more lighting to counteract the lower reflection given by the darker ceiling.

Manufacturers and shelter magazines offer a wealth of color schemes for the bathroom. Each incorporates the brand-name fixture color to keep you from going astray. Should you decide to "strike out on your own" in selecting a new color scheme, first obtain a Color Wheel from a local art store. It puts colors in relationship to each other so that you can see for yourself which colors you like. Here are a few color tips from American-Standard designers:

—COMPLEMENTARY COLORS: You can decorate with colors that are opposites on the color wheel ("complementary" colors): red and green; blue and orange; yellow and violet. If you choose a complementary color scheme, don't use both colors at full strength, or intensity. For instance, with a vivid red, use a dark, greyed green. For a strong purple, bring in a pale gold, not butter yellow.

—ANALOGOUS COLORS: You can use colors that are next to each other on the color wheel, "analogous" or "adjacent" colors: orange, yellow-orange, and yellow; green, yellow-green, and yellow; violet, red-violet, and blue-violet. These color schemes are vibrant, and usually great fun to work out.

Bold shapes and bright colors add a mod flavoring to this free-form bathroom. Three steps up to the shower area give the square-shaped tub a sunken appearance. Both the water closet and bidet are one-piece fixtures. The island lavatory is served by a mirror suspended from the ceiling on brass rods. Kohler photo.

Bright, bold colors straight from the flag highlight this lavatory setting by Kohler. The wash basin is antique red, the toilet New Orleans blue, and the shag rug bold red. The bright blue of the fixture is repeated in shag carpeting used as a wall covering between the red-and-white stripe vinyl wallpaper.

—MONOCHROMATIC COLORS: You may decide to use only one color in varying shades and intensities; this is called "monochromatic" colors, and can be one of the easiest and often most effective types of color plans. Everything is tied together by the bond of color. For instance, a blue bathroom could include a blue bathtub with pale sky blue, delphinium blue, and a touch of navy blue for accent. Monochromatic schemes resemble music—many variations on a theme.

—NATURE'S COLORS: Keep in mind that there are no discordant colors in nature. Blue and green are always together. A color scheme can be built from a flower, a bowl of fresh fruit, a basket of vegetables, the shades of a mottled rock formation. Your catalyst for a color scheme might be a fabric or a print: a gay chintz or a provincial print could key everything else in the room.

3 Walls, Ceilings, Floors, and Plumbing Systems

Walls and Ceilings

Wall surfaces in the bathroom should be moisture resistant and easy to maintain. Because most bathrooms are fairly small, it is best to use the same wall covering throughout. This is not a positive rule, however, as can be seen in many of the photographs illustrating this book.

In choosing bathroom wall surfacing, it is a good idea to select a material, color, or pattern compatible with the decorating scheme used in adjoining rooms. This can be accomplished with color, textures, and choice of materials. Wall surfaces commonly found in bathrooms include decorative plastic laminates, ceramic tile, plastic tile, enamel-painted plaster or gypsum wallboard, and vinyl wall coverings. Wallpaper and fabric can be purchased with a washable and waterproof surface, or waterproof treatment can be applied following installation. Generally, wallpaper is more practical in lavatories and powder rooms where moisture is not produced by tub or shower bathing.

Most bathroom walls are finished in pastel or light colors. If you wish to use a dark color or a simulated dark wood finish, keep in mind that this will absorb more natural and artificial light. You may need additional lighting to compensate for the dark walls. The most critical wall area in the bathroom is that around a tub or shower stall. When tile is to be applied, vinyl-surfaced gypsum wallboard, waterproof plaster, or marine plywood is first applied to the framing. The vinyl wallboard comes in one piece that can be scored to fit around three sides of the tub, but in shower stalls this material must be carefully taped at all seams.

Both plastic and ceramic tile should be applied with water-resistant adhesives. Plastic laminates and predecorated tempered hardboard are also used for tub and shower area walls and, again, special care should be given to obtaining leak-proof joints.

Decorative Plastic Laminates

Decorative high-pressure laminated plastic has become one of the most frequently used materials in today's bathroom. This durable product is suitable for countertop surfaces, walls, bathtub surrounds, and as a vertical surfacing for many decorator-styled vanities and cabinets.

Laminated plastic was developed in the early 1900's as an electrical insulating material. Decorative plastic laminate was born when the top layer of paper in the laminate "sandwich" was printed with a design before being bonded into the plastic. The design, visible through the transparent plastic-resin surface, provides the material's beauty. Today's decorative plastic laminate is available in literally hundreds of solid colors, wood grains, patterns, and a variety of textured and three-dimensional surfaces; it provides virtually unlimited design possibilities.

Laminated plastic surfaces are almost abuse-proof in normal use. They are easily cared for with a damp cloth and retain their beauty year after year with no refinishing required. The material in also available in a "cigarette proof" grade. Impacts that dent wood, and cuts, scratches, and abrasions that mar paints and lacquers, hardly affect laminated plastic. The material is manufactured in large sheets that can be cut to fit most any shape. Large areas may be covered with seamless or almost seamless surfaces, and by using "postforming" techniques common to cabinet makers,

Redi-Set pregrouted ceramic tile sheets, approximately two square feet, are easily put into place over gypsum wallboard. The grout joints are filled at the factory with a flexible silicone rubber grout which will not mildew, stain or crack out with building movement. After all sheets are in place, the same grout material is used to finish the installation. American Olean photo.

laminated plastics may also be applied to many curved surfaces.

Ceramic Tile

Ceramic tile's popularity as a covering for bathroom floors and walls is due to its beauty, ease of maintenance, and resistance to water. Produced by mixing clays that are baked at extremely high temperature, the material comes in several forms.

GLAZED TILE is composed of metallic oxides and ceramic stains which give the tile surface color and texture. This kind of tile can be found in sizes ranging from 1 inch square to 12 inches square, and in a vast variety of shapes. Colors range over the entire palette, with the very bright colors less resistant to wear. Gloss, matte, and crystalline glazes are suitable for interior walls and vanity tops. Crystalline and certain other glazes may also be used on floors. Thicknesses are available from 3/8 to 5/16 of an inch. Installation costs will range from $1.30 to $4 per square foot for 4-1/4-inch tile, depending upon the method of installation and size of the job. The more elaborate shapes and designs may cost as high as $10 per square foot installed.

CERAMIC MOSAICS are usually small unglazed solid chunks with color in the body of the tile. They come in sizes 1 × 1, 1 × 2 and 2 × 2 inches. A broad color choice exists, affording great design flexibility with this unit size, which may be combined in many patterns and colors. The only limitation on design is imagination. The average thickness is 1/4 inch. The ceramics are usually mounted into sheets measuring 1 × 2 foot, either on paper or back-mounted. Ceramic mosaics are suitable for interior and exterior floors and walls. The porcelain type will absorb less than 1/2 percent moisture, is frost-proof, and highly wear resistant. The natural clay type has a rich, natural appearance but is more porous and more likely to stain. These tiles need never be waxed, but a sealer is sometimes used to protect the cement joints. Cost of installation will vary from $1.50 to $3.15 per square foot, depending upon cost of tile (varying with color, size and designs) and method of installation, with an average of $1.75 to $2 per square foot.

An authentic reproduction of Appalachian slate has been used for the tub wall, lavatory countertop, and side walls of this bathroom setting. The new decorative plastic laminate from Evans Products Co. contrasts with Conestoga Butterfield paneling.

Material combinations in today's bathrooms often include natural wood, ceramic tile, decorative plastic laminates, flexible vinyl, plastics and carpeting. Each plays an important role in minimizing upkeep as well as adding to the overall decor. American-Standard photo.

QUARRY TILE comes in warm, earthy shades, generally ranging from beige to dark, rich brown. The tiles are usually unglazed, and the color is integral throughout the tile body. Some manufacturers incorporate a color stain. Sizes range from 4 × 4 inches to 8 × 8 inches and a number of shapes are available, including hexagon, octagon, and provincial. Quarry tile is usually 1/2 inch thick and is made by the extrusion process from natural clay or shale. Quarry tile is suitable for residential floors and is highly resistant to wear from abrasion. Originally used primarily in commercial installations, quarry tile is now used extensively in homes because its warm, natural tone lends itself to either the contemporary or provincial look. Cost of installation will range from $1.65 to $3.25 per square foot. Curved, special shapes are more time-consuming to install and will cost slightly more.

Ceramic tile can be installed over previous ceramic tile as illustrated here. The "before" view shows mildewed and cracked grout. Following the preparation of the surface (by cleaning all soap film and hard water deposits off the existing tile), adhesive is spread with a notched trowel and pregrouted sheets applied. New grout lines created between adjoining tile panels are caulked with silicone rubber grout which is highly stain and mildew resistant. It also is flexible and will not crack or deteriorate.

Linen Stripe 16 inch by 8 foot prefinished planks were used in this bathroom remodeling project. Like all Marlite paneling, Linen Stripe has a washable plastic finish, resists hard wear, heat, moisture, and stains. Tongue-and-groove edges simplify installation with concealed clips and adhesive.

Washable vinyl in a newspaper pattern adds an amusing touch to this bathroom. The white "spice" pattern window shade by Breneman and matching valance have crimson trimming to pick up the accents in the pictures and hand towels. Photo courtesy of the Window Shade Manufacturers Association. (Opposite)

Royaltile panels by Masonite can be applied to any solid backing such as plaster, plywood or drywall for both new construction and remodeling. A special "Tubkit" includes everything needed to renew the area. Additional matching panels may be used for the balance of the room as shown here. Many patterns offered.

Decorative rough-hewn wood beams and wood parquet flooring are augmented by wood shutters and vanity in this master bathroom. Washable pull drapes are used for the fiberglass shower recess as well as the water closet compartment. Universal-Rundle photo.

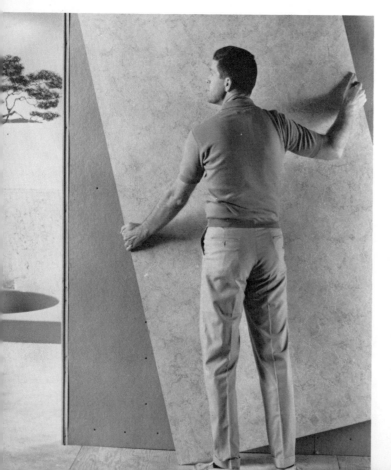

Textured paneling that can be damp-wiped clean may be used for remodeling or for new construction. The plastic-finished hardboard goes up quickly over old walls or any solid backing. The 1/8-inch thick Marlite panels are 4 × 8-feet and come in numerous colors and patterns.

Z-Brick, an all-mineral decorative brick, gives the appearance of the real thing without the cost or difficulty of traditional bricklaying. Available in several styles and a variety of colors, the material is applied with a hacksaw, file, trowel and small brush. It is completely fireproof and waterproof.

Vinyl and plastic laminate patterns used for wall surfaces can be repeated in custom vanity door designs to create an interesting effect. A solid-color plastic laminate countertop has recessed bowl.

Antique elegance achieved in this remodeled bathroom flaunts a stained glass window and crystal chandellier. The ceiling has washable drop-in panels in a metal grid while the washable walls have a marble-like finish. Marlite photo.

Daylighting a bathroom via the ceiling skylight is an approach being used by more and more architects and builders. Standard acrylic and glass domes are available for use on flat or pitched roofs. Usually framed in corrosion-resistant aluminum, these domes can be clear and colorless, white and translucent and dense white, depending upon the light diffusion desired. Wasco Products photo. (Opposite)

Luminous ceilings are popular in the bathroom as well as the modern kitchen. The wall-to-wall units can be easily formed to match the room shape and diffuse even illumination throughout the area. A metal grid attached to the ceiling supports the removable plastic panels. Wasco Products photo.

Resilient floor tile can be installed over concrete or wood subfloor. Waterproof adhesive should be used for all resilient materials.

A pressure-sensitive asbestos felt sheet system for installation of ceramic tile eliminates, in many cases, the need for mastic, thin-set mortar, or epoxy adhesive. The four-square-foot sheets may be used with glazed tile, ceramic mosaics, and quarry tile, and can be applied over plywood, concrete, existing ceramic tile, hardwood floors, or resilient flooring if sound. American Olean photo.

FLOORS

Resilient Flooring

Bathroom floors are subjected to water and moisture and therefore should be surfaced with materials that resist water. Resilient flooring (in tile or roll form), ceramic tile, and carpeting are the flooring materials most commonly used in bathrooms.

Careful attention should be given to acquiring and installing resilient flooring. When the location is on or below grade level, you may choose from asphalt, vinyl-asbestos, rubber and solid vinyl. Use linoleum only above grade to avoid moisture problems. In all applications, a waterproof adhesive is specified. Use of sheet materials is preferred by many homeowners. This material is the least susceptible to moisture seepage because sheet goods can be coved and installed with a minimum number of seams.

Asphalt tile is the least expensive tile material and costs approximately one-third the installed price of rubber or vinyl tile. Vinyl-asbestos tile has a coating of clear plastic that wears well. This material is priced between asphalt and vinyl tile. Ceramic tile can be laid at grade or above grade level in the usual way and grouting applied. When installing any type of tile, be sure to purchase several extra pieces for possible future replacement. Patterns and glazes available change and often it is impossible to match colors a few years after installation.

Nylon and olefin (polypropylene) are the most commonly used types of carpeting for bathrooms. Both resist soil and moisture and are long-wearing. Carpets of olefin fiber are virtually stain-proof while providing the functional benefits of warmth, noise reduction and beauty. The fabric can be easily maintained because soil remains basically on the surface of the fiber and does not penetrate.

In a small bathroom, a light-colored floor looks larger and more unbroken than a dark or patterned floor. Unless the bathroom is unusually large, it is better to avoid borders of a different color. The closer all the bathroom surfaces are to each other in color, the larger and more unified the room will appear. When selecting plumbing fixtures, manufacturers can provide you with color charts to help you determine compatible colors for room surfaces and accessories.

Plumbing Systems

When it comes to planning the plumbing for a new or remodeled bathroom, your best course of action is to place yourself in the hands of a competent plumbing contractor. Most builders and architects planning new home developments carefully review floor plans with their plumbing contractor, or even with a plumbing engineer, to determine the most economical arrangement. This is especially true if the basic floor plan will be repeated many times throughout a multi-home development or an apartment complex.

The basic "mechanical core" of your plumbing system is installed in the wall and floor of the room. It consists of vents, traps, waste lines and soil stacks, and hot and cold water supply lines. Basically, there are two types of plumbing systems—that which is totally fabricated at the site, and that which is prefabricated off-site, trucked to the job and dropped into position, often before the roof of the home is put in place.

Various types of prefabricated systems are available. One type, for example, is a core unit which combines a complete kitchen and bathroom in a single modular package. All fixtures and appliances are factory-installed and the total unit is set in place with a crane ready for hook-up to supply and waste piping. Another type of prefabricated system is the so-called "plumbing tree" which provides drain, waste, vent, and supply lines all tied together. This unit also is set in place before the roof goes on the home. It is engineered to the specific floor plan and is fabricated with materials to meet specific local building code requirements. Still another variation of the plumbing tree used in some areas of the country is a unit which provides a four-foot "half-wall" including horizontal piping only. The vertical plumbing is then installed at the job site to complete the installation.

Four major types of pipe are used in residential plumbing systems—copper, galvanized iron, cast iron, and plastic, the latter in two types, polyvinyl chloride (PVC) and acrylonitrile butadine styrene (ABS). Regional and local building and plumbing codes detail where and when each type may be used. Some local codes do not permit plumbing by persons other than licensed contractors.

Although most plumbing systems are based upon national codes, your local building code concerning plumbing may vary from the code in an adjoining city or town. Therefore, it is wise to check the code beforehand in making any major change. Generally speaking, your plumber will be most familiar with what you can and cannot do as regulated by local codes.

According to the National Association of Home Builders, cast iron is the most widely used pipe for drain, waste, and vent systems. Plastic pipe is second in preference, followed by copper and galvanized iron. Copper is the material most often used for supply lines, followed by galvanized iron and plastic.

Lower weight and easier fabrication has caused many builders and plumbers to favor plastic piping for DWV (drain-waste-vent) systems. For example, identical plumbing trees for one installation show this variation in weights:

- cast iron weighing 156 pounds
- copper at 35 pounds
- plastic at 20 pounds

From the standpoint of time, it takes about one minute to make a joint in a 3-inch PVC stack, far quicker than with cast iron.

Residential plumbing systems, both prefabricated and site-fabricated, connect to city sewerage, septic tanks or cesspools for disposal. The most common city sewer system includes all drain lines, including rain water and sanitary, taking all disposable materials away from the property.

Septic tanks are watertight receptacles which receive the discharge of the drainage system or part thereof. They are designed and constructed to retain solids, digest organic matter through a period of retention and allow the liquids to discharge into the soil outside of the tank through a system of open-joint piping or a seepage pit built to conform to the plumbing code. Septic tanks are built of metal or cast concrete and require cleaning every two or three years on the average. However, these tanks should be inspected annually, preferably in the Spring of the year.

A cesspool is a lined excavation in the ground which receives the discharge of the drainage system and is designed so as to retain the organic matter and solids discharging therein, but permitting the liquids to seep through the bottom and sides. Cesspools are usually constructed of hollow concerete block or stone.

Waste lines and soil stacks connect with the plumbing fixtures in the bathroom or lavatory, making it possible for waste to flow to the main disposal system of your home, the sewer or septic tank. The waste piping is smaller in diameter than the main soil pipe buried in your yard. Relocation of waste lines and soil stacks

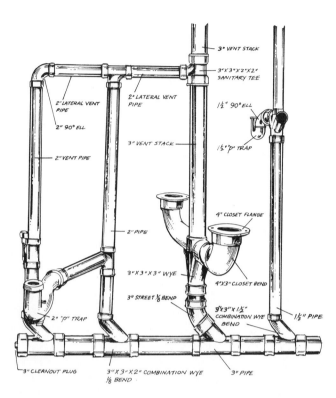

PLASTIC PIPE DWV SYSTEM shown here was assembled with all PVC pipe and fittings at a savings of approximately 70% when compared with metal pipe and fittings. Note the 3-inch vent stack which permits standard 2 × 4 stud wall construction. Larger 4-inch stacks require greater wall thickness.

in bathroom remodeling can be very costly and in some instances virtually impossible. In homes with concrete slab flooring, for example, the waste lines and soil stacks are embedded in concrete and would have to be cut out if relocation of fixtures were desired. In homes with crawl space or sufficient area under the bathroom floor, these lines can be relocated, but even then it is expensive to do so.

The typical residential plumbing system consists of these basic components:

—SOIL STACK, a 3 or 4-inch pipe which runs vertically from the lowest point in the system to six or more inches above the roof line where it is flashed for protection from the weather. The stack may extend more than one story and when equipped with aerator fittings (for self-venting), a single stack can be used for waste and vent plumbing in multi-story buildings such as apart-

ments. Two stacks can be tied together at the top above the highest fixture with only one stack extending through the roof line.

—DRAIN PIPES, usually 1-1/2 inches minimum to accommodate bathtubs, shower stalls, lavatories and laundry trays. Also called "branches," these pipes are joined into the vertical soil stack. While lavatories can be adequately drained with 1-1/2-inch branches, water closets require a minimum soil branch size of 3 inches, and both bathtubs and shower stalls are best served by 2-inch waste branches. It might also be noted that water closets should be located with a minimum of 15 inches of area from the center of the fixture to the wall or cabinets at each side. A minimum space of 24 inches should be allowed from the front rim of the water closet to the facing wall surface.

—VENT STACKS, providing for a flow of air to or from a drainage system or forcing a circulation of air within the system to protect trap seals from siphonage and back pressure. Vent stacks are usually 2 inches in size and run from the horizontal drain line at the base to an intersection in the vertical soil stack. This latter connection must be at least 6 inches above the overflow rim of the uppermost fixture served. Vent stacks continue through the roof line and may be no closer than 10 feet to a window, door, opening, air intake or ventilating shaft. The vents must be 10 feet above the ground level and 6 inches above the roof line. The vent must also be at least 3 feet in every direction from any lot line. Fixtures without vents can, under certain conditions, siphon water from the traps and allow the sewer gases to enter the room.

—SUPPLY LINES, typically 1/2-inch copper pipe with hot water line installed vertically a minimum of 6 inches to the left of cold water line when faucet side is viewed from the front. Lines from the outdoor meter to the water heater are generally 1 inch to 3/4 inch in diameter.

—TRAPS, curved pipe or tubing shaped like the letters "S" or "P" which, when properly vented, produce a liquid seal which will prevent the back passage of air without materially affecting the flow of sewage or waste water through it. Approved connections are measured from the trap to vent along a horizontal line, except a water closet or bidet, which is measured to include the developed distance from the top of the floor flange to the inner edge of the vent.

Limits established for the distance between trap and vent in continuous waste and vent systems include the following for residential applications:

- 2'6" maximum for one fixture using 1-1/4" pipe (usually for lavatories)
- 3'6" maximum for bathtubs, laundry trays using 1-1/2" pipe
- 5'0" maximum for shower stall or floor drain using 2" pipe
- 6'0" maximum for floor drain using 3" pipe
- 10'0" maximum for floor drain using 4" pipe

The maximum pitch on any trap arm is 1/4 inch per foot.

It is well to check the available water pressure when installing an additional bathroom. One way to do this is to turn on several faucets in the house for a few minutes. If the pressure falls off noticeably, the outside water supply may be inadequate. Larger pipes may be needed to make up for it. Another factor to consider in remodeling a bathroom or adding another is the size of your water heater and its recovery rate. The average 2-1/2-bathroom house with an automatic washer and/or dishwasher requires at least a 50-gallon hot water tank, and a 60 or 72-gallon unit is recommended to insure adequate hot water for normal household use.

Light is directed onto the washbasin by flanking lamps, rather than reflecting from mirror. Eljer Sauna photo.

Light from flower-petal lamp catches gleam of smooth tile in this sleek, compact design. American Olean Tile photo.

4 Lighting for the Bathroom

Regardless of size or shape, every bathroom needs two types of lighting—general and directed. In a very small bathroom or powder room, a single light in the ceiling or above the mirror or medicine cabinet may provide sufficient general and directed lighting, but mirror side lights are also recommended. Lighting engineers recommend 30 footcandles of illumination for the bathroom. This is the equivalent of 3.5 to 4 watts of incandescent lighting per square foot of floor area, or 1.5 to 2 watts of fluorescent lighting.

The greatest need for directed lighting in the bathroom is for shaving and make-up. A ceiling fixture above the mirror and a light fixture on each side of the mirror will illuminate the face without shadows. All three fixtures are usually wired to and controlled by one wall switch. As described in the "Accessories" chapter of this book, combination overhead lighting units complete with exhaust fans and heater elements may also be used. These units often are controlled by a wall timer, especially the fan and heater functions.

Another popular ceiling treatment is the wall-to-wall or large-area luminous ceiling with fluorescent tubes installed above removable plastic panels suspended in a metal or wood ceiling grid. This type installation provides a more even distribution of lighting throughout the room.

Incandescent lamps are generally preferred for use in areas where women apply make-up as this type of illumination is most like sunlight in color. Always choose white bulbs for bathroom use, as tinted bulbs or shades distort colors. When one or more lavatory basins are installed in a vanity countertop more than four feet wide, several 75-watt incandescent bulbs or two rows of fluorescent tubes above the mirror in a soffit at least 15 inches from front to back will give even, adequate illumination.

Vapor-proof fixtures are recommended for use in tub and shower areas, and in the case of the tub, should provide sufficient light for reading. Electrical outlets should be carefully placed in the bathroom to accommodate the use of an electric razor, hair dryers, electric comb, toothbrush, etc. These outlets, of course, should be grounded.

Here are some basic "rules of lighting" as set down by General Electric experts:

LIGHTING SMALL MIRRORS: Use three fixtures, wired to one switch.

Incandescent. Ceiling unit should be centered over the front edge of the lavatory bowl or countertop. The fixture should be a minimum 12-inch diameter with two 60-watt bulbs. Wall brackets should be centered on the mirror, 30 inches apart and 60 inches above the floor. At the minimum a 6-inch diameter should have one 75-watt each, and preferable for a 5 to 6-inch diameter, spacing should be 16 to 24 inches with two 60-watt or four 40-watt bulbs. Pendants of equal or greater diameter should be similarly spaced.

Fluorescent. Use deluxe warm white tubes with trigger start ballasts, located and wired to one switch. Ceiling fluorescents should be two to four-tube units (20 watt) 24 inches in length and shielded. Fluorescent 20-watt wall-bracket units should flank the mirror with the center of the tube located 60 inches above the floor.

LIGHTING LARGE MIRRORS: Mirrors 36 inches or greater in width should be illuminated with a double row of deluxe warm white (30-watt, 36 inch; or 40-watt, 48 inch) fluorescent tubes in a recessed fixture or custom built into a soffit. Recommended soffit dimensions: 16 inches front to back; 8 inches deep; full length of counter.

Translucent plastic panels conceal four 40-watt fluorescent tubes in this wood-framed luminous ceiling. The plastic panels are easily removed for re-lamping and may be washed off in bathtub or shower. Carriage lamps double as night lights. It would have been better to place the mirror 8 inches above the counter to prevent splash marks.

THEATRICAL EFFECT: Exposed-lamp fixtures across the top and sides of a mirror should include four to six lamps per fixture. Decorative 15 watt or 25 watt bulbs are recommended. Side strips should be 30 inches apart.

Lighting in separate compartments of the bathroom should be a minimum one 75-watt, R-30 type unit recessed in the ceiling, or 8-inch diameter 100-watt surface mounted fixture or wall bracket. Fixtures used in the shower or tub area should be recessed vapor-proof type for 75 or 100-watt, with a switch outside of shower area. A bathroom night light can be either a 15-watt switched wall bracket or plug-in type units with 4 or 7-watt bulb. Sunlamps should be equipped with a timing device. Infrared heatlamps should be used in U/L-approved fixtures.

Recessed valence lighting and decorative side light fixtures illuminate mirror medicine cabinets from three angles. Countertop and backsplash are decorative plastic laminate (Adjacent and opposite below)

Soffit lighting is enhanced by an L-shaped mirror arrangement in this bathroom, which incorporates the three most used bathroom materials—wood, ceramic tile and decorative plastic laminate. American Olean photo.

5 Bathtubs and Surrounds

Bathtubs in Many Sizes, Shapes, Types

Today's bathtub has come a long way from the wooden or galvanized tub originally brought from the side porch to the center of the kitchen on long-ago Saturday nights. Instead of the Spartan dunking ritual, we now have bathtubs designed for comfort and stretch-out relaxation.

Color is making the traditional white tub a fixture of the past, just as modern design is adding an elegance heretofore not found in the bathroom. Major manufacturers now produce a great selection of bathtub styles, sizes and shapes to meet almost every conceivable bathroom plan.

THE RECTANGULAR TUB, a standby for better than a half century, ranges from 4 to 6 feet in length, is just under 3 feet in width and is 12 to 16 inches high. Sloping backs, body-contour designs, slip-resistant bottoms and safety-grip handles are among the latest features. Many units have a convenient integral seat that can easily double as a handy tub-side shelf for soaps and toiletries.

THE SQUARE TUB, is typically 31 to 48 inches long, 42 to 49 inches wide and 12 to 16 inches high. This fixture, installed in a recessed area or corner, can solve the problem of limited space. The square tub doubles very well as a shower receptor.

THE SUNKEN TUB, more popular each year as greater emphasis is placed on good bathroom design. This type of installation can be either a custom-design fixture created with ceramic tile, or a factory-made fixture produced for "sinking" in the floor or a raised platform.

One manufacturer's version of the sunken bath is a steeping model which measures 15-1/8" deep, nearly 6-1/2 inches deeper than most conventional tubs. With arm rests incorporated into the interior design of the tub, this model provides a high degree of reclining comfort. Another steeping-type tub on the market has a 55 × 37 inch interior to accommodate two persons, side by side. This unit fits into a standard 5-foot width area and uses standard fittings.

Most bathtubs on the market are manufactured from one of three materials—molded cast iron with a porcelain enamel surface; formed steel with a porcelain enamel surface; or a molded gel-coated glass-fiber-reinforced polyester resin commonly known as "fiberglass."

The cast iron tub dates to 1870, while enameling can be traced to ancient Egyptians and Assyrians. These tubs are the heaviest, weighing from 200 to 500 pounds, with a 1/16-inch (approximate) coating of porcelain. They are also the least susceptible to damage.

Formed steel tubs weigh but 100 pounds and thus are generally preferred for remodeling purposes as well as for use on upper floors of homes and apartments. These units feature the same porcelain enamel finish as cast iron, but are less costly. Two types are manufactured: one-piece with integral apron (front); and two-

Kohler's steeping bath is 20 inches deep, almost six inches more than most five-foot bathtubs, and offers deep-down soaking. A three-foot width and gently sloping back provide added comfort. Safety features include grip handles and slip-resistant bottom. This tub has a "no-apron" design for installation in a corner, island or peninsula setting, or in a recess, virtually at any level. The tub comes in 13 colors.

Slip-resistant surfaces are now being built into many conventional bathtubs such as this American-Standard model. Safety stick-ons also are available in skid-resistant vinyl to update older tubs and shower floors.

piece with a separate apron which is welded into place before the enameling process. The evident welded seam may be offensive to some buyers. Manufacturers offer a sound-deadening coating for both styles of formed steel tubs and the reasonable cost is usually justified by the resulting reduction of shower noise.

Fiberglass tubs are the newest development, with the units in widespread use since around 1968. Lightweight yet durable, these units come in a wide range of colors and in many instances incorporate surrounding panels which form a tub-shower combination. Oval-shape designs are now quite common in fiberglass tubs and 5-foot length is by far the most popular size. These molded, one-piece units can incorporate arm rests, integral seats, and shelves. They are kept clean with a sponge or cloth and liquid detergent; users are cautioned to use only manufacturer-approved cleaners for this purpose (see "Maintenance").

American-Standard's Gothic Pool is one of the firm's oversized bathing tubs made of fiberglass-reinforced polyster. The unit is big enough for two persons and has a built-in seat which doubles as an accessory holder. The tub comes in six colors.

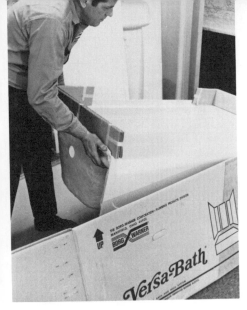

The four-piece Versa Bath by Borg-Warner includes tub and three wall panels in a single carton.

The bath unit and wall panels are secured directly to the wall studs with ordinary wood screws and patented fasters.

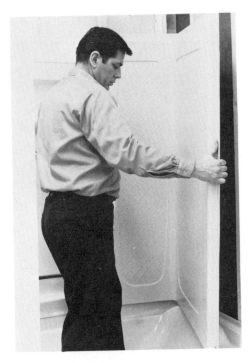

The L-shaped end panels are positioned after the center panel is in place, and the outside edge again fastened with screws.

The four-piece fiberglass Versa Bath by Borg-Warner can be used for remodeling or for new construction. Installation is said to require only 90 minutes following preparation of the five-foot bath alcove, stripping of floors and walls, positioning of water and drain pipes, and installation of key studs. The Versa Bath can be supplied for right or left-hand drain, and fully assembled is 74-1/2 inches high, 60 inches long and 31-1/2 inches front-to-back. Shower doors may be attached directly to the tub panels.

The center wall panel is put in place following the leveling and securing of the bath unit.

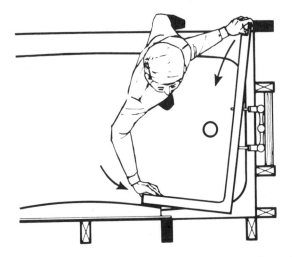

Overhead view shows the positioning of the end panel, which has been drilled to accept plumbing supply.

Less than an hour's time is required to install a glazed ceramic tile bathtub surround called the System 310. The wainscot-height, 49-square-foot package consists of eight pregrouted sheets of tile, with trim attached, and two internal cove corner strips which allow for a 5/8-inch variation in size of the tub recess. The system can be installed over properly sealed gypsum wallboard, concrete masonry, plywood or gypsum plaster. It's waterproof, and highly stain- and mildew-resistant. The entire tub surround is packaged in two cartons. The silicone rubber used in the factory grouting is also used for perimeter grouting and sealing at installation time. The only cutting required is for pipe holes and for tub "legs." Manufactured by American Olean Tile Co., System 310 is available in seven stock colors, and may be had in other shades on a special-order basis. Matching tile base is also available in pregrouted 32-inch strips. The system is compatible with other Redi-Set tiling sheets used for other areas of the bath. All feature noncracking grout.

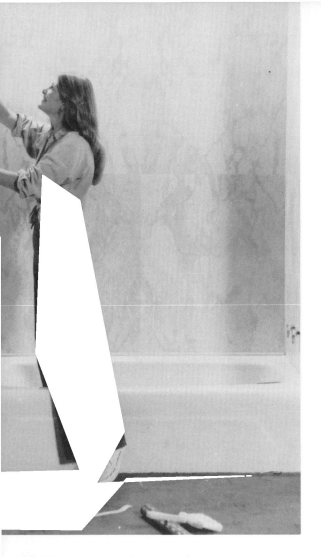

Tub Recess Kit Speeds Remodeling

Marlite tub recess kits available nationally from local building materials dealers simplify the job of updating an older bath. The kits contain all the necessary materials for the job and offer a selection of panel colors and patterns including a South Pacific and Catalina mural panel for the center area. The "complete bath in a box" kit includes one 5 × 6-foot and two 30-inch by 6-foot panels with precut harmonizing moldings, caulking, nails, and how-to-install booklet, with or without adhesive and spreader. Adhesive is furnished.

Installing the tub recess begins (Figure 1) by establishing guidelines for edge molding, and by caulking the tub rim along the wall. Tub moldings are installed. The second step calls for fitting the back panel (Figure 2), caulking tub moldings, coating the back of the panel with adhesive and placing it on the wall. The top edge molding is then fitted and applied. With the back panel in place, one end panel (Figure 3) is fitted and openings cut for plumbing outlets and handles. Caulk is applied to the tub and corner moldings, the panel is coated on the back with adhesive and placed on the wall. Edge moldings are fitted and applied. The remaining panel (Figure 4) is applied in the same manner (without cutting holes), plumbing fixtures and handles are replaced, and the excess adhesive removed with white gasoline to complete the installation.

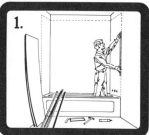

Corian bathtub wall kit by DuPont consists of two end panels, two back corner panels and a center wall strip which overlaps the two back panels to provide a sculptured effect. The panels are 1/4-inch thick and 57 inches high. Corian is also available for countertops and can be purchased as an integral one-piece top and bowl.

6 Shower Stalls and Doors

Shower Stalls

Shower stalls can be custom fabricated during construction of a new bathroom or they can be purchased in prefabricated form from various manufacturers in a wide range of sizes and styles. All shower stalls require care and attention during installation to prevent possible leakage which can rot the area under the shower and surrounding framework.

Factory-made, one-piece units, are obviously the quickest and easiest to install in both new construction and remodeling. However, remodeling often requires three-piece or four-piece units which can be moved into an existing area via a doorway which would not be big enough to permit passage of a one-piece, fully assembled unit.

Gel-coated fiberglass bath-showers are offered in colors to coordinate with lavatories and toilets. The units often incorporate built-in seats for sit-down showering, and corner ledges for soaps and toiletries, ilt-in grab bars and nonslip bases.

Another feature of the one-piece tub-shower com- n is the smooth, easy-to-maintain wall surface iminates 50 square feet or more of wallboard an r panels. The unbroken surface prevents possib ks and there are no joints or grout lines to keep cle

Fiberglass hower stalls range in size from 32 × 32 to 53-1/2 × 38-3/4 inches. Heights range from 75 to 90 inches. The units may be fitted with rod and shower curtain or conventional shower doors. Metal shower stalls finished with baked enamel or vitreous porcelain enamel also are widely used in remodeling. The units are designed so that all joints between panels are flanged to interlock with one another for easy waterproofing. Floors of these units are precast to provide floor, threshold and curb. Reinforced plastic or precast terrazzo are generally used.

Clay tile is most often used for custom-installed shower stalls, but other waterproofed surfacing materials are also satisfactory. Careful attention should be given to waterproofing all joints.

Standard sizes range from 32 × 32 to 40 × 40 inches. Standard trim includes brass mixing valves, shower head, soap dish, vinyl curtain, and curtain rings. Shower doors are usually optional. While the custom shower can be any desired size, standard floor receptors for this purpose come in such dimensions as 32 × 32, 36 × 36, 48 × 32, 54 × 33 and 40 × 40-inch corner models. Likewise, the floor may be fabricated of clay tile with a subsurface shower pan made of sheet lead, copper, or waterproof and damp-proof membrane formed to the desired size and shape. The membrane material is a lamination of heavy paper and asphalt reinforced with glass fibers and costs considerably less than sheet lead or copper.

When planning a custom-designed shower, it is well to consult with your contractor or plumber to make sure that construction will conform with local building and sanitation codes.

Depending upon the final design of the shower stall, it may require a waterproof light fixture, or it may be lighted by fixtures elsewhere in the room.

Standard location of grab bars is 48 inches above the floor, while soap dishes should be recessed 54 inches from the floor. Shower head location varies from 60 to 66 inches from the floor and may incorporate a personal shower head for localized bathing and simplified cleanup. Single-handle mixing valves are preferred in the shower for added safety in dialing the desired water temperature. Use of an exhaust fan in the ceiling of the shower will remove steam.

Open-area garden-type showers can be created with a wide selection of glazed and unglazed wall tile and ceramics ala this Franciscan Hermosa setting. Note the lowered dress table area with hamper doubling as seat.

Shower receptors such as this 34 × 48-inch Surfline by American-Standard are often used in combination with ceramic tile in creating custom shower stalls. The premolded units eliminate the need for bulky lead pans.

Molded shower floors are available in various sizes and are manufactured with nonporous and nonslip surfaces. The one-piece units can be installed faster and at a lower cost than the custom lead pans often used in the construction of ceramic tile showers.

Tub-Master's model FSI folding shower door installs on the inside of metal and nonmetal shower stalls, not between the jambs. The door folds neatly behind the returns for complete unobstructed access to this Fiat shower.

Tub-Master's "B" Series shower doors are rigid bypassing units that also fold by simply unhooking the outside towel bar and inside grab bar. The design permits both doors to fold into small stacks at either end for complete tub-shower access. The doors come in a wide range of decorator colors.

Biscayne model shower doors by Shower Shield are
framed in smooth, bright anodized silver or gold
aluminum. Tracks are self-draining. Aside from this
two-door model the firm produces neo-angle units,
stationary panels, and hinged doors for shower stalls.

Cabanabath II, a one-piece fiberglass tub-shower unit
by Universal-Rundle, has an optional top which
eliminates the need to finish the wall or ceiling area.
The unit is 80 inches high, compared to the traditional
72-inch height. The top increases the overall unit to
the standard 84 inches. The unit comes in a selection
of colors and is fire-retardant.

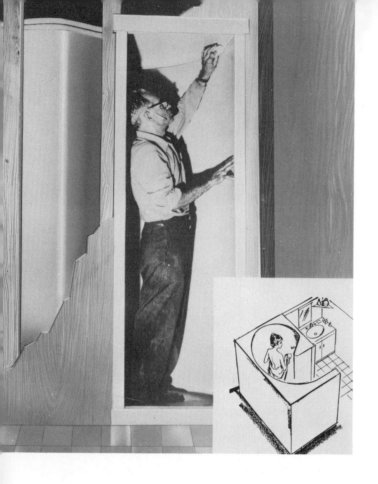

A shell design for the Swan fiberglass shower eliminates doors and curtains as well as water on the floor. Units are shipped knocked down for ease of assembly. Designer-selected colors are available.

Shower Enclosures

Bath enclosures, shower enclosures and shower doors are manufactured in two basic types—rigid aluminum framed units, and flexible folding models. Both styles are offered in all standard sizes and can be ordered in custom sizes as well.

Rigid enclosures vary in size from the single-door swing model to the by-passing double-door type used with bathtubs. Frames are of extruded aluminum while panels are tempered glass or 3/16 inch plastic in a choice of clear or colors. The sliding units operate on nylon rollers and feature self-draining tracks. Width-wide handles on many units may be used for towel racks.

The flexible folding shower door and enclosure usually have the same anodized silver or gold aluminum frame as the rigid-type unit and provide the added feature of nearly full access to the tub or shower when folded back to a mere 8 to 10 inches. This type of enclosure is made of high impact polystyrene, which will not shatter and is easy to maintain. Folding units are offered in a wide range of colors and decorator designs and can be installed in about 30 minutes. Available models in many instances are keyed to the catalog number of major manufacturers of bathtubs and showers to enable a perfect fit.

Before-and-after views illustrate the see-through mirror type bathtub enclosure manufactured by Sierracin/Agalite Bronson. Available in shower stall and tub models, the Mirage is transparent on one side and a mirrored surface on the other. The unit offers privacy for the bather without obstructing vision. The glass is made to the same specification as automobile windows and is four to six times stronger than ordinary glass. The hardware is gold anodized aluminum.

7 Lavatories

The lavatory (or bathroom sink) offers the greatest possible selection when it comes to designing a new bathroom or remodeling an existing one. There are many styles, shapes and sizes offered in a choice of vitreous china, cast iron, formed steel and plastic. In determining your needs, it is wise to first select the specific type of lavatory you wish from the five basic styles offered:

FLUSH MOUNT, a unit which requires a metal ring or frame to hold it in place in the plastic laminate or tile countertop. One problem faced with this type installation is keeping the rim joint clean.

SELF-RIMMING, a style which eliminates the metal framing rim as it rests on the countertop, overlapping the mounting hole which is normally cut by the countertop fabricator at the specified location.

UNDER-THE-COUNTER, this unit is secured under the surface of the countertop by means of metal fasteners. The countertop opening corresponds to the shape of the bowl. These tops are usually plastic laminate, marble or a simulated "synthetic" marble. There are problems in keeping the underside clean, especially at the joint line.

INTEGRAL LAVATORY-COUNTERTOP, again, usually of synthetic marble or plastic, the one-piece units are seamless and easily cleaned. The entire unit rests on the cabinet framework and has predrilled holes for fittings.

WALL-HUNG, the conventional unit known to most persons from childhood on. This type is secured to the wall, juts out from it, leaves plumbing pipes exposed and provides no storage. It is the least expensive and requires the least space.

Lavatory shapes include rectangular, round, ovals, shell designs, angles, swirls and triangular. Some units are designed for placement of the lavatory fittings on the bowl rim while others require installation of fittings in the surrounding countertop area.

Oval lavatory basins measure from 17 to 19 inches across the front and 14 to 16 inches front to back. Some designs have extra deep bowls for doing hand laundry and are not apt to cause splashing. Being rounded, they clean somewhat faster than fixtures with corners.

Circular lavatory basins are 18 to 19 inches in top diameter and approximately 13 inches bottom diameter by 12 inches deep. Designed for installation in a 21-inch or wider countertop, some of these fixtures have concealed front overflows and antisplash rims.

Triangular units come in dimensions such as 11 × 11, 16 × 16, 17 × 17 and 18 × 18 inches for use in corners or rooms where space is at a real premium. These units have a back ledge which provides space for soap and a water tumbler. Projection into the room is approximately 4 inches greater than the triangular edge dimension.

Specialty lavatories available from national manufacturers include "his" and "her" shampoo and grooming centers incorporating built-in spray arms and swing-away faucet spouts. One "her" version doubles as a miniature bathtub for bathing the baby.

Standard height for installation of lavatories is 31 inches from the floor to the top of the basin rim, but units can be installed from 34 to 38 inches off the floor if they are to be used by adults only. An 8-inch space is recommended between the top of the lavatory and the bottom of the mirror or medicine cabinet installed above.

When lavatory basins are to be used in pairs in a countertop, a minimum of 12 inches should be

Gerber lavatory bowls for bath or powder room feature a lifetime pattern for an unusual decorative effect. The pattern may be in black or gold, and the bowl may be self-rimming or undercounter style. Standard size is 19 × 16 inches.

The European flavor in bathroom fixtures is shown in this white china pedestal washstand with gold trimming from the Sherle Wagner collection. Semi-precious jeweled faucets are in rose quartz set in 24-carat goldplate.

A front self-draining soap rest is conveniently located below the lavatory rim of this vitreous china fixture from Borg-Warner Plumbing Products. Also featured is a hidden overflow drain.

Designed for cramped-for-space bathrooms and powder rooms, the Botique lavatory from Kohler measures only 21 × 13 inches and can be used in a countertop as narrow as 15 inches from front to back.

A concealed front overflow is a feature of the Briggs Marlowe 19 × 16-inch oval bowl. Designed for undercounter installation, the bowl is available in white and decorator colors.

Washbasins of museum caliber, decorated by hand with all the richness of enamel and bas-relief, are available from Sherle Wagner. In the $100 to $250 range, these fixtures in Delft, Meissen, Lowestoft and classical Chinese designs are matched by similar designs for door knobs, drawer pulls, soap dishes, paperholders, wallpaper and other accessories.

provided between adjoining fixture edges. For more elbow room when two people use adjoining basins, a 20-inch space between fixture edges is more satisfactory if space permits. The lavatory should be no closer than 6 to 8 inches from the side edge of the countertop to provide a small ledge and prevent splashing on the floor. Location of basins at extreme ends of an L-shaped countertop is one method of providing for ample elbow room. Distance from the front of lavatories should be a minimum of 20 inches to the opposite wall or to a fixture on it.

The self-rimming Rondelle lavatory by Kohler is a vitreous china fixture with sculptured basin. The unit is 21 × 19 inches.

Just 18 inches in diameter, this American-Standard self-rimming stainless steel lavatory has a satin finish bowl, brass outlets and is installed here with acrylic handled fittings.

Lady Vanity is Kohler's multi-purpose lavatory for bathroom or bedroom. It serves equally well as shampoo lavatory, beauty care center, miniature bath for bathing babies, or laundry basin for washing nylon hosiery and delicate garments. The unit measures 28 × 19 inches and has a 23 × 14-inch sloping basin with swing-away spout and handy shampoo spray attachment.

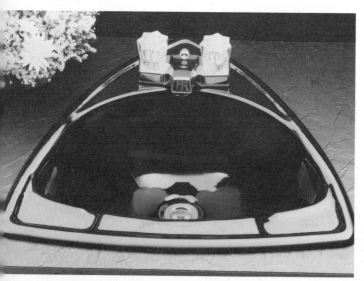

Briggs Cathedral lavatory is a three-sided, self-rimming unit that adapts to corner countertop installation in a small room. Overall dimensions are 19 1/2 × 18 3/4 inches.

A powder room ensemble available from Borg-Warner includes provincial vanity cabinet, cultured marble one-piece lavatory, gold-tone faucet and drain assembly, and matching toilet flush handle.

Universal-Rundle's Mediterranean style vanity is shown here with the firm's 24-inch drop-on cultured marble bowl top. The white-on-white unit has a raised soap dish that swirls into the bowl.

Offered in 12 colors, American-Standard's Oval Contura (left below) is a lightweight plastic lavatory said to be chip free, stain resistant and rustproof. It comes with 4 or 8 inch centers, measures 20 × 17 inches and has a depth of 6-1/8 inches.

Designated the Man's Lav by Kohler (right below), this 28 × 19-inch cast iron fixture has built-in disposer for soap or lotion and spray shampoo fitting in addition to conventional water controls and faucet. The self-rimming lavatory is installed here in a plastic laminate countertop.

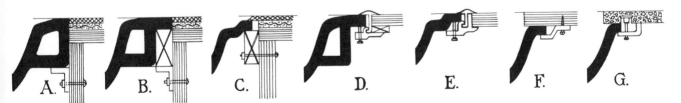

A.   B.   C.   D.   E.   F.   G.

RECESSING A LAVATORY can be accomplished by various means depending upon the type of countertop selected. Diagrams A, B and C show lavatory bowls joined with ceramic tile countertops; D, E and F are set in decorative plastic laminate; G is set in marble.

8 Bathroom Vanities and Countertops

Bathroom vanities add the appeal of fine furniture to bath and powder room settings and can be arranged in a virtually endless variety of combinations. Stock and custom units are offered with or without countertops and basins, affording the purchaser a wide degree of design flexibility.

While most bathroom installations include a bowl unit, combinations may be formed without a bowl unit for installation in dressing room, bedroom, hallway or other area of the home. Most units are modular in size to simplify planning and installation, but for rooms with odd dimensions, an exact fit can be accomplished with filler strips.

Standard cabinet units are available in widths of 12, 15, 18, 21, 24, 30, 36, and 48 inches. Front-to-wall dimension varies from 17 to 21 inches while the standard height is 29-1/2 inches, minus top. Units include a 4-inch kick space. Vanity bases are manufactured with one, two or more doors and may be purchased with drawers right, left or flanking the doors. Still additional arrangements are possible through custom arrangement. Drawers are available in both wood and plastic molded design while hardware, including knobs, pulls and self-closing hinges, is styled to give the desired effect.

Among the most popular styles of vanities being installed in new homes and in remodeled rooms are Early American, Spanish, Mediterranean, White & Gold, Provincial, and Contemporary. Nearly all feature carved doors or fronts reflecting the skill of cabinetmakers. Aside from natural wood, today's vanities are manufactured in a wide range of decorative plastic laminates which require virtually no upkeep. This durable material comes in solid colors, decorative patterns, and rich wood grains.

Countertops

Bathroom countertops generally are restricted to areas where decorator-style vanities are used, but in some cases the tops are also used for shelf-style installations, surrounds of tubs, and other areas where visible storage and utility are desired. Three types of materials are basic to most installations—decorative high-pressure plastic laminate (such as the well-known Formica), ceramic tile, and marble or synthetic marble. By far, plastic laminates are the most used throughout the United States, but in some regional areas tile predominates.

Manufacturers of decorative plastic laminates recommend their 1/16 inch-thick material for all horizontal applications and caution that their 1/32 inch material should be confined to vertical applications such as walls and cabinet fronts. Plastic laminates open a wide range of design opportunities to those planning a new or remodeled bathroom. They come in literally hundreds of colors, patterns and wood grains, as well as new "leather" and "slate" three-dimensional textures.

Countertop fabricators use two terms to identify the types of bathroom countertops they offer: self-edged and postformed. The first term designates flat tops with a square front and a separate edging of the same material. The backsplash is again a separate piece with a square inside corner. Postformed plastic laminate countertops are made of a single piece of the material, formed to provide a flat surface with rounded front edge and curved backsplash. This type surface has no joints to collect dirt and is easy to maintain.

Ceramic tile is available in a wealth of colors, sizes, and types for countertop installations as well as for

Color-fast white finish of NuTone's Montreal vanities is protected by a clear acrylic finish to prevent yellowing. Nontarnish gold edging and scrollwork are triple-sealed against flaking, chipping and fading. Durable plastic laminate countertops in gold color were used in this master bathroom.

walls, floors, showers and other areas of the bathroom. This hardy material is installed at the site, atop a specially prepared base stock affixed to the prefabricated vanity unit.

Among the most popular ceramic tile countertops are:

GLAZED TILE, offered in hundreds of colors, has a smooth finish, and is impervious to heat, grease, spots and spills.

CRYSTALLINE AND SCORED TILE, has a textured surface, usually gives the appearance of smaller tile as opposed to conventional 4-1/4-inch tiles. This type can also be used on floors and walls.

MOSAICS, solid and textured colors, form a smooth, dense surface. Many distinctive patterns offered.

QUARRY TILE, unglazed, exceptionally rugged, is usually used for floors. Mostly "earthy" tones.

DECORATED TILE, used primarily for "spot" applications in glazed surfaces, creates a focal point. Hundreds of designs available.

Marble and synthetic marble countertops, installed as single-piece slabs, are resistant to scratches, mars, and stains, and are easily maintained.

DuPont's Corian is manufactured in Cameo White and two marble pattern colors, Dawn Beige and Olive Mist. The non-porous material can be worked much like wood and can be fabricated with power tools. Standard sheets are offered in three thicknesses—1/4 inch in 30 inch width and in lengths of 57, 72 and 98 inches; 1/2 and 3/4 inch in 25 or 30-inch width, and in lengths of 98 and 121 inches.

Federal oak, once so common in residential ice boxes, is used for a Haas line of bathroom and powder room vanities. Oak paneling and decorative plastic laminate countertop complement this setting.

Manufactured bathroom vanity cabinets provide for numerous layout arrangements including this one-wall design featuring NuTone's Devon line. The dressing table area has its own immediate storage drawers yet is separated from the wash bowl area by a handy linen closet. Matching wall cabinets above the bowl are used for medicines.

Provincial door styling of these Triangle Pacific vanity doors is enhanced by a light patterned decorative plastic laminate used for the countertop. Floor-to-ceiling linen closets flank bowls to provide added storage area.

Connor Winchester model vanities have solid furniture fronts, core stock with hardwood oak veneer face and back. All parts are machined for blind mortise and tenon, or dadoed and sanded for fit, then glued and pinned together.

Contempory vanities from Formco in white walnut, Spanish oak, avocado oak and harvest gold have self-closing hinges and are finished inside and out with washable vinyl. The 12 × 36 inch matching medicine cabinets are surface-mounted.

Classic Harvest vanities by Haas Cabinet Co. are modular in design to custom fit any area. Fine furniture woods are protected by a patented finish that resists scratches and stains.

Twin-bowl installation in Early-American style vanity provides ample area for two persons. The countertop is made of synthetic marble. Haas Cabinet Co.

Kiln-dried hardwood is used in the manufacture of Triangle Pacific's bathroom vanities. This Canterbury design incorporates twin lavatory bowls and mirrors. The countertop is plastic laminate. Shallow medicine cabinet is built into the divider wall.

Deep relief Spanish doors in oak or walnut set the style for the Formco Espanol vanity line. Bases are modular and available in two-door units of 24, 30 and 36 inches; the 36-inch unit is available in a 3-door unit with three hidden drawers right or left side behind the third door.

Molded louvered-style doors and washable vinyl interior simplify day-to-day maintenance of Classic Manor vanities and matching wall cabinets from Formco. Units are offered in white walnut and cherry finish.

Mediterranean style vanities by Long-Bell have plank-style doors accented with antique brass-finished hardware. Matching cabinets have been used for a dressing table reflected in the mirror.

9 Water Closets and Bidets

Considerable design improvements have been made in recent years in the manufacture of toilets, or water closets, as they are known in the trade. These units are not all alike—some work better than others, some are quieter than others and some are more attractive than others. Plumbing engineers for many years have been trying to design a toilet with completely noiseless flushing action, but to date none have succeeded. However, the degree of noise is reduced substantially as the toilets range from the lowest-priced "washdown" model to the highest-priced "siphon action."

Most residential toilets consist of a bowl and a tank, with the tank providing sufficient water storage to create a proper flushing action in the bowl. While most toilets are floor mounted, wall-hung units are available to provide for easier floor maintenance. Basically, water closets are offered in four basic models (see drawings), each distinguished by its different flushing action:

THE WASHDOWN is the noisiest and least efficient. No longer acceptable in many areas, this unit is flushed by a simple wash-out action and tends to clog more easily than other models. Another disadvantage is that much of the bowl area is not covered by water and is therefore subject to fouling, staining, and contamination. Most major manufacturers have removed this type of water closet from their lines.

THE REVERSE TRAP units are less noisy than washdown models and are the least expensive of the siphon-action toilets. Similar in appearance to better siphon jet action toilets, these units have a smaller water area, passageway, and water seal. They are flushed by creating a siphon action in the trapway, assisted by a water jet located at the inlet to the trapway. This siphon pulls the waste from the bowl. The reverse-trap toilet is more sanitary than the washdown model since water covers more of the bowl surface.

THE SIPHON JET type of toilet is quieter than the washdown or reverse trap and has a larger water surface with most of the interior surface of the bowl covered with water. Generally more expensive than the reverse trap model, the siphon jet has a larger trapway (it must pass a 2-1/8-inch ball) which is less subject to clogging.

THE SIPHON ACTION low-profile, one-piece toilet is the "top of the line" and least noisy of all types of toilets. This model has almost no dry surfaces on the bowl interior and the trapway must pass a 2 inch ball. Another feature is the low profile design sought in many bathroom layouts.

Regardless of the type of toilet selected for new construction, remodeling, or replacement, the unit must perform a full cycle of functions:

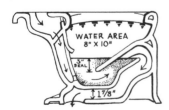

The Washdown

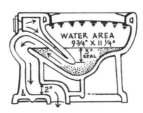

Reverse Trap

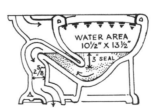

Siphon Jet

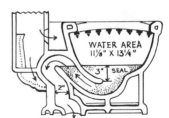

Siphon Low-Profile

The Bolton agua-vent toilet with elongated bowl from Kohler uses a pressurized spray in the flushing action to remove unpleasant odors. The mechanism is contained within the toilet and requires no special valves or pipes.

The Cadet Water-Saver by American-Standard can be flushed with a third less water than conventional siphon-jet units.

- flush completely and efficiently
- shut off the water flow to the bowl at the end of the flushing action
- refill the tank to the necessary depth and then shut off the water supply line

Tank mechanisms will vary from manufacturer to manufacturer, but most units operate with a ballcock attached to a valve by means of a rod or arm. As the toilet handle is pushed, the water flows from the tank to the toilet as the ballcock drops and the valve opens. As the tank refills, the float ball rises, closing the valve and stopping the flow of incoming water at the proper level indicated by a mark inside the tank. Manufacturers caution that homeowners not set the tank water level below the indicated mark in an effort to save water. A reduced volume of water is likely to provide an incomplete flush and not cleanse the bowl.

Toilet styles vary somewhat from maker to maker, but most have round or elongated bowls. The latter style is sometimes referred to as "extended rim" and is approximately 2 inches longer front-to-back. The elongated is more comfortable, more attractive, and easier to keep clean.

Wall-hung, off-the-floor toilets usually require 2 × 6-inch wall studding instead of the usual 2 × 4 inches. These units are supported by heavy steel carriers installed inside the wall and are hidden from view in the finished installation.

Still another variation in toilets is the triangular tank model which conserves floor space when installed in a corner area normally wasted. A 24 × 24-inch corner accommodates most such units.

The Bidet

The bidet was first conceived and used in Europe as a hygienic plumbing fixture which provided a high degree of cleanliness. Today's bidet is merely a low-set bowl that is no more complicated to use than any other fixture found in the bathroom.

The bidet user sits astride the fixture facing the hot and cold water faucets (on the bowl or wall) to wash the pelvic and anal areas. The faucets operate the same as lavatory bowl fittings, controlling both water temperature and pressure. The fresh water enters the bidet either through an upward water spray in the center of the bowl, or through a flushing rim which helps to maintain bowl cleanliness.

Typical dimensions of the bidet are 13-1/2 inches wide, 25 inches back-to-front and 14 inches high. Units should be installed in an area 30 inches wide or wider and with a minimum of 18 inches front clearance between fixture and wall.

Most bidets on the market today incorporate a stopper which retains water in the bowl if desired. The purpose of this is to use the bowl for foot soaking.

The Rochelle one-piece water closet is Kohler's top-of-the-line model and provides virtually silent flushing action. It comes in a wide choice of colors.

The American-Standard toilet is a one-piece unit with low, unobtrusive tank. The fixture is available with Vent-Away, a water system which creates a vacuum in the bowl, drawing air and odors through holes in the flushing rim into the discharge outlet of the toilet, and into the vent pipe.

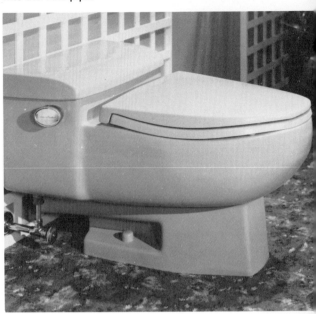

Wall-hung water closets simplify floor and fixture cleaning. This elongated Glenwall from American-Standard is equipped with a Vent/Away ventilator which automatically eliminates toilet odors before they can become bathroom odors.

Thermo-Tank by Universal-Rundle Corp. is made of ABS injection-molded plastic and has a corner flush tab which replaces the conventional flush lever. The tank is preassembled and preadjusted, so no on-site work is necessary. The tank contains an inner liner that prevents condensation even under very humid conditions.

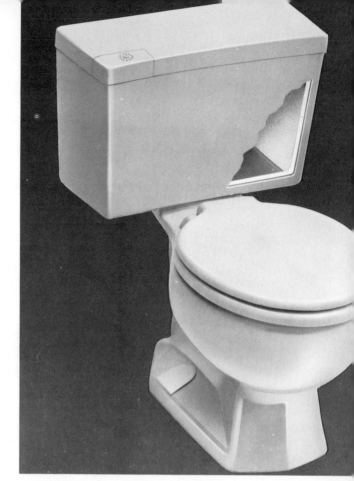

Eljer's one-piece Silette vitreous china water closet combination with rounded front bowl and ultra quiet flushing action has been combined in this installation with the firm's Barcelona 22 × 15 inch bidet. Cabinet contains storage area, control panel for bidet fittings, and small open shelf.

A new vitreous china finish called Earthen Stone is being used in the manufacture of toilets and self-rimming lavatories available from Borg-Warner Plumbing Products. The stone finish comes in topaz, jade and slate. The finish is a smooth ceramic glaze for easy maintenance.

American-Standard's Margate bidet matches in color and styling any toilet in the company's line. The bidet is equipped with pop-up drain for filling the bowl with warm water as well as a spray. Water control knobs are located at eye level.

Kohler's Caravelle bidet is sold as a companion fixture to the Rochelle closet. Both fixtures are offered in deeptone and pastel colors including "Black Black." Bidet features include fittings located on a recessed shelf at the rear of the fixture, hidden supply lines, and working parts.

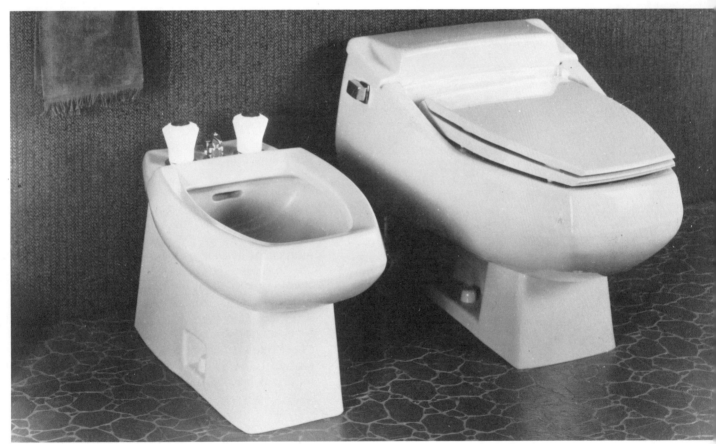

Toilet Seats

A toilet seat can help establish the decor for the entire bathroom and thus should be selected for more than its functional purpose. Seats are manufactured in molded wood with baked-on enamel, as well as solid molded plastic. Matching colors are available for most nationally distributed fixtures.

The shape of the toilet seat you select will be determined by the shape of the water closet itself—round or elongated bowl. The lid may be "full size" to "close"

the front, or it may be slightly smaller, closing back a bit from the edge of the seat itself.

Aside from the matching or contrasting color and plain white, today's toilet seat can be obtained with a marbelized finish, scuptured wood cover, golden scroll design, American Beauty Rose inset, Coat of Arms, and other decorative designs. Look for coated metal corrosion-resistant hinge posts in selecting a toilet seat. You may also wish a seat with an easily removed hinge to simplify bowl and seat cleaning.

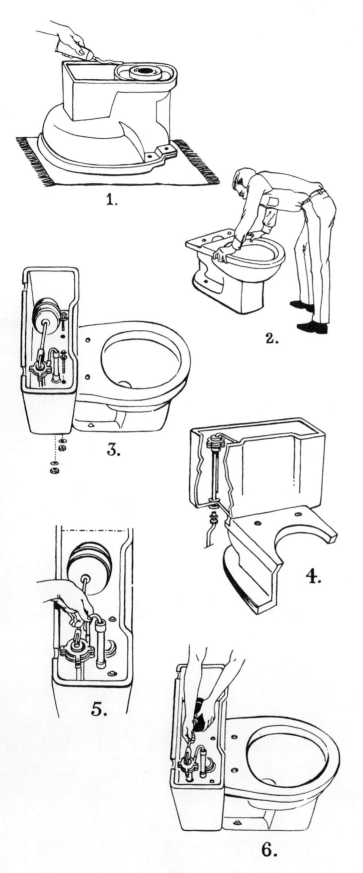

1.

2.

3.

4.

5.

6.

Installing the Toilet Tank and Bowl

Replacement of an existing toilet tank and bowl or installation of this fixture in a new bathroom begins with a thoroughly clean floor surface where the bowl is to be located.

The fixture is placed upside down on a protective soft material to prevent scratching (Figure 1) and a warmed wax ring applied to the circular recess in the base of the bowl. This is where the fixture will be connected to the waste line previously plumbed through the floor. A setting compound is then applied to the outer rim of the bowl to assure a continuous seal to the floor.

The bowl is then carefully set atop a metal flange previously attached to the floor. The toilet bolts fit through holes in the base of the fixture (Figure 2) ready to receive washers and nuts which should be secured snugly. They should not be force-tightened.

Following placement of large donut-shaped washers on the threaded tank outlet, the tank is placed on the ledge (Figure 3) of the bowl and aligned for placement of bolts downward through the bolt holes of the two parts. Again the bolts should be carefully tightened, alternating from side to side to prevent breaking the tank or bowl.

The cold water line is then connected to the tank with a straight or angle stop (Figure 4), and the ballcock inserted into the tank and secured in position. This later unit (Figure 5) varies in style with appropriate installation instructions detailed on the package.

Water is turned on by opening the angle or straight stop located beneath the tank. The tank should fill to the "water line" indicated inside the tank. If not, the brass rod supporting the float ball (Figure 6) should be bent until the tank stops filling at the water line. Check the maintenance section of this book for a cut-away view of the ballcock mechanism used in most toilet tank installations.

10 Saunas and Steam Baths

Saunas

More and more American families are making the sauna bath an integral part of their home, and many of these installations are coupled with the master or family bathroom. Discovered by the Finnish over a thousand years ago, the sauna is a convenient way to shed the tensions of modern living and relax tired muscles.

Most modern saunas are prefabricated units which can be quickly assembled in a variety of sizes to accommodate from one to four or more persons. Custom-made units also can be built to the buyer's specifications. Prices generally run from $450 to $1500 or more.

Many Scandinavian families have relied upon the sauna for generations, considering it almost as essential to their well being as food or drink. Finnish athletes to this day insist upon having saunas in their Olympic Games quarters.

The traditional Finnish sauna was a small detached building, heated with a wood-stoked furnace piled high with stones to retain and radiate heat. It often took eight or nine hours to reach the desired 175 to 200 degree F (or hotter) temperature.

A modern sauna can be made ready in 15 minutes or less and provides fully automatic temperature control. In the American version, humidity is held to 8% or less, making the high temperatures comfortable. Some units contain rocks, onto which you pour a few drops of water for a touch of high humidity at the end of the sauna.

Although the Finns use aspen wood, kiln-dried clear all-heart and A-grade redwood is an adequate substitute for the modern-day sauna because of its ability to

Family-sized saunas by Viking come complete with insulated walls and ceiling, floor, carpet, heater, sauna stones, electrical controls, door, light and benches. A patented locking device is built into the panels to eliminate the need for nails, screws and bolts in the on-site assembly.

Fasco saunas feature modularized construction, are shipped knocked-down for easy assembly. The package includes benches, door hardware, heater, wood trim, slatted platform floor, interior light fixture, insulated door and deluxe controls.

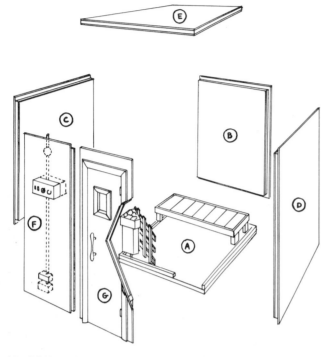

Prefabricated saunas consist of insulated panels (designated A through F) and a preassembled door (G). The heat control panel is built into panel F for fast connection to existing power source.

withstand extreme temperature changes. Redwood acts as an insulator on the walls, ceiling and floor. It diffuses the heat so the surfaces remain warm but not hot to the touch (unless they get wet).

Location of a sauna in a home should be convenient to a shower or swimming pool, as sauna bathing requires cold water dousing as the final step. Some families have located the unit in a separate outbuilding, an unused bedroom, a closet, basement or remodeled storage room. Others have added on a sauna bath to their homes adjacent to a bathroom or as part of a cabana adjoining a swimming pool.

Standard packaged-type saunas on the market range in size from 3'4" × 3'4" to 8' × 12' and have an inside height of 6'6". Depending upon size, the units come with one to five benches and will accommodate up to 18 persons. Custom designs can be ordered prefabricated for fast assembly at the site. Free-standing floor and wall-mounted electric heaters vary in wattage from 5200 to 15,000, depending upon room size. The UL-listed units are operated by remote controls, or in the case of two smaller models on the market, the heater and controls are built into the door.

The Steam Bath

Steam bathing, or as it is often called, "Turkish bathing," has a long history. Hippocrates, Father of Medicine, reportedly used steam baths in the treatment of fever in 395 B.C. The Greeks considered it a vital part of their rigorous physical education program and the steam bath formed an integral part of the famed Greek gymnasia. This Grecian devotion to steam bathing was adopted from ancient Egyptians who first incorporated bathing into the medical arts.

Today the steam bath is much in vogue although the public Turkish baths which flourished in the 1920 and 1930's have given way to private steam bathing. Units on the market can be installed in a vanity or in the ceiling of a bathroom, or anywhere up to 50 feet away from the tub or shower. No special enclosure is required to create a steam room. Vapor-proof and shatterproof sliding glass doors are simply installed to seal the existing bathtub or shower, which becomes the steam cabinet.

Steam bathing and sauna bathing are two separate concepts. The sauna is a high-temperature, low-humidity treatment (usually a maximum of 15 percent humidity). The steam bath, on the other hand, has a high moisture

Am-Finn saunas are prefabricated and prepackaged in four sizes to occupy 24, 40, 64 and 80 square feet of floor space and to accommodate from three to fifteen persons. The units can be assembled and ready for use in a few hours, requiring no need of block wall or studding. Wall and roof panels are of "sandwich" design with poured-in-place polyurethane insulating core. Clear heart redwood is used for the interior walls, floor and ceiling. The residential application pictured here occupies a former walk-in clothes closet.

Solo saunas by Viking fit practically anywhere. The prefabricated units are 3'4" × 3'4" and stand 6'8" high. Heater, controls, light and Vent-Window are built into the door. This sauna operates off any standard 120 volt, 20 amp fused circuit.

Thermosol converts any tub or shower into a professional, private steam room. The system consists of: (1) electronic steam generator; (2) anti-scald steam outlet head (inside enclosure); (3) timer control and operating instructions; (4) fold-away plastic seat (or stool for tub installation); panels and tub enclosure; and (6) complete waterproofing of the bath area. The generator can be located up to 50 feet away from the shower or tub.

ULTRA SAUNA PRECUT ROOMS

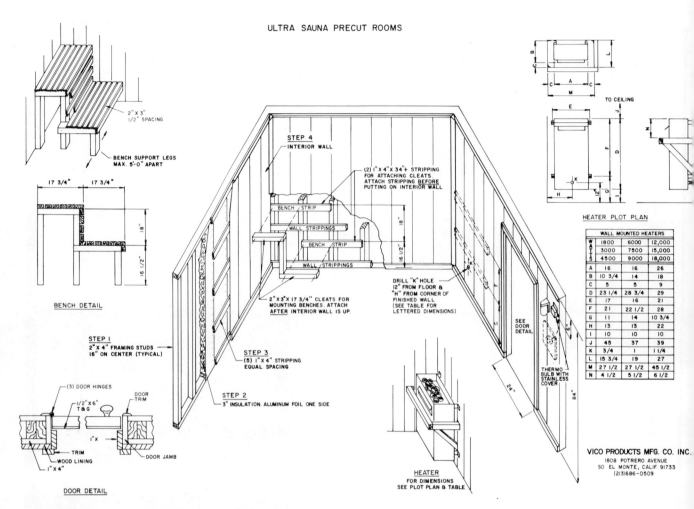

WALL MOUNTED HEATERS		
1800	6000	12,000
3000	7500	15,000
4500	9000	18,000
A 16	16	26
B 10 3/4	14	18
C 5	5	9
D 23 1/4	28 3/4	29
E 17	16	21
F 21	22 1/2	28
G 11	14	10 3/4
H 13	13	22
I 10	10	10
J 45	37	39
K 3/4	1	1 1/4
L 15 3/4	19	27
M 27 1/2	27 1/2	45 1/2
N 4 1/2	5 1/2	6 1/2

VICO PRODUCTS MFG. CO. INC.
1808 POTRERO AVENUE
SO. EL MONTE, CALIF. 91733
(213)686-0509

This model by Vico, called the Ultra Sauna, comes with precut panels and a variety of optional accessories, such as benches, backrests, heaters, and control panels. The above plan shows dimensions for different size saunas, and materials.

content with its average humidity level of nearly 100 percent. The average steam bath is 10 to 20 minutes, followed by a lukewarm or cold shower. Such baths cleanse the skin and invigorate the system. Steam generated for the bath is easily condensed to water by turning on the regular shower.

The mini-electronic steam generator referred to is no larger than a breadbox and is controlled by a timer or thermostat set by the bather. Steam is produced within three minutes, and gradually raises the temperature between 70 and 160 degrees, as desired. The only visible equipment is a steam head, which does not interfere with the normal use of tub or shower.

Model floor plans, depending on area size and plumbing available. A Vico Products photo.

11 Bathroom Fittings

Bathroom fittings undoubtedly receive more constant usage than any other bathroom feature. Faucets, spigots, taps, centersets, combinations, shower heads—they are all designed to control or direct the flow of water as well as to contribute to the room decor.

Fittings add the finishing touch to every plumbing fixture and should be selected with care. Some lavatory fittings are priced under $25, while others sell for more than $100 per setting. It is advisable to purchase known brands and avoid off-brands and "bargain" fittings because of the difficulty in securing replacement parts in later years.

Most manufacturers produce fittings in three price ranges, low cost, middle price, and a luxury line. Most buyers find the best-for-the-money to be the middle price units, but others who desire the luxury aspect are willing to pay more for the decorative appearance. Lower-priced fittings often can be the most expensive in the long term. The price of fittings depends upon the quality of brass used in their manufacture and the internal operating mechanism. Most fittings now available use all-brass construction in basic parts as this material offers maximum resistance to corrosion and is not affected by strong detergents, alkalinity, or salt air. While most faucets are bright chrome, there are gold faucets, china faucets and faucets made of colorful plastics. Each creates its own atmosphere and may be selected to enhance the total decorative scheme.

There are two basic types of lavatory fittings: centersets and spread fittings. The centersets are one-piece units combining faucet and single-handle or double-handle controls for water supply. These units are designed for installation in single-hole bowls and in units with two holes four inches apart. The spread-type fitting consists of separate handles for hot and cold water supply and a faucet for installation in lavatories with two holes 8 to 12 inches apart. This type of fitting is more expensive than the 4-inch centerset fitting. Each handle and faucet is installed according to the hole arrangement of the lavatory or can be built into the countertop when a recessed bowl is specified.

Shower Controls

The two-valve fitting is the most common shower arrangement with each handle being turned individually to adjust flow of hot or cold water and the blending of both to the desired temperature. The newer single-control valve operates by either knobs or levers which can be moved upward or downward, or in and out, to control volume. The same control is moved to the left or right to control water temperature.

Still newer yet is the pressure-balancing valve which is usually preset to a temperature which is then automatically maintained regardless of the decrease of flow of either the hot or cold water. With this unit, should the pressure of the cold water supply drop sufficiently to cause scalding, the valve automatically shuts off the hot water flow. This type of valve is most commonly used for controlling a showerhead.

A fourth classification of fittings is the thermostatic control which incorporates a heat-sensing device to automatically adjust the hot and cold volume to maintain a preselected temperature of mixed water. This valve gives a more precise temperature control than the pressure-balancing valve, and it usually permits the user to control volume as well as temperature.

Shower Heads

In selecting a shower head, choose a self-cleaning unit that thoroughly flushes the interior of the head with water to prevent possible clogging. If the shower

The Alsons Shower Spa system provides liquid soap, bath oil, or skin conditioner at the turn of a dial; dial again and fresh water is supplied via the flexible-arm fitting which can be moved up and down the wall bar to suit height of user.

The inner nozzle on the Rain Jet rotates in an oscillating orbit, discharging streams of swirling, activated water to provide a "massage" during your shower. The cone section slides forward to change the water pattern from wide to bubbly.

head does become clogged, you can unscrew it and clean it by hand.

Most shower heads now on the market are also equipped with a small knob which can be easily finger-adjusted to select the desired water flow—including needle, rain, flood (for shampooing), and gentle. One particular model even provides a water massage by discharging streams of swirling, activated water.

Standard shower heads are equipped with ball joint swivel connections to permit simple direction. More expensive units also feature automatic flow control to limit the amount of water used per minute. This latter type unit is especially desirable in areas of high water costs.

The newest type of shower head offered for both new construction and remodeling is the personal shower accessory which may be used attached to the wall as a conventional shower head as well as hand-held. Equipped with a chrome-plated flexible hose approximately 5 feet in length, this accessory provides controlled body spray, simplifies clean-up, permits localized bathing, is fine for bathing pets, and permits a woman to shower without getting her hair wet.

Toilet Tank Fitting

Another important accessory for the bathroom is an all-brass fitting which mixes hot and cold water delivered to the toilet tank and bowl. This unit can be installed under the closet tank, under the floor or near the water heater to provide water of near room temperature, thus preventing condensation during humid weather. The unit works in any climate. It might be added that some water closets on the market feature an insulation lining inside the tank to prevent condensation.

For ease of servicing or emergency, all plumbing fixtures should be installed with supply line cut-off valves. Should you need to turn off the water to replace a lavatory washer, for example, you merely twist the valve handle under the bowl without turning off the main valve to the house. Access to cut-off valves for bathtub-shower units should also be provided so that they can be turned off. These valves often will be in the wall or in a closet or room adjoining the bathroom. It's a good idea to know where your cut-off valves are and how they work so you can reach them easily and quickly in case of emergency.

Crystal is very much back in the bathroom, both for single-handle and two-handle faucet controls. These units by Bradley carry 1000-month warranties against leaks.

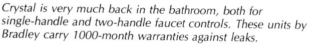

Gerber faucet ensembles come in both spread (illustrated) and centerset styles, in a wide selection of lead crystal, satin gold, lustrous pewter and satin chrome. Matching styles are available for tub and shower applications.

Push-pull or single-lever operation is optional with Kohler's Centura lavatory fitting. The push-pull model (top) has pentagonal acrylic handle. Single-lever model offers finger-tip operation. Both models use dependable cartridge inside.

Selecting a Faucet for Your Bathroom

A visit to your local buildings materials dealer or plumber will quickly inform you that not all faucets are the same. Not only do they come in brushed and polished finishes, they also differ in size, shape and the basic way they work inside.

There are faucets with two handles and there are faucets with a single handle. The more traditional two-handle sets operate by simply turning on one handle for cold water and the other for hot water. To get a mixture, you use both handles and the more you "open" them, the greater the flow of water produced.

Kohler's Raindrop personal shower has a two-way diverter valve installed before the conventional showerhead to let you switch from showerhead to Raindrop and back again. Raindrop personal shower comes off the wall for hand-held localized bathing, shampooing, bathing children, or showering without getting your hair wet. Kohler's Rite-Temp pressure balanced mixing valve maintains water temperature regardless of pressure changes in the supply line.

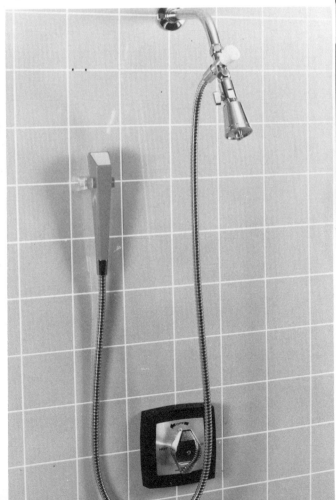

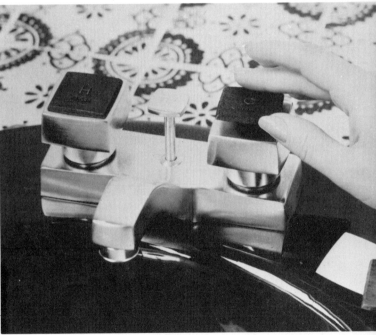

Antique lavatory fittings by Kohler are available in brushed or polished chrome or gold electroplate. Mounting is on 12-inch centers, adjustable to 8-inch centers.

Interchangeable accent color inserts for the handles of lavatory, bathtub and bidet add to the decorating possibilities of Alterna fittings by Kohler. Four pairs of inserts come with each fitting and can be changed quickly and easily.

The Ultra Font lavatory faucet by American-Standard provides a soft upward arc of water that falls into the bowl without splashing. The unit doubles as a drinking fountain, aids in shampooing and lingerie rinsing. Fluted acrylic handles control water supply and temperature. The faucet comes in 24-karat gold plate, gleaming chrome, and stain-chrome.

The Moenique by Moen combines a single-handle shower control with safety grab bar, soap dish, shampoo shelf, and shower-tub diverter. Bather pulls on the dial for water, turns to right or left for temperature changes.

Powers Hydroguard "400" control and fixture set is polished chrome-on-brass. Second from the left is the pressure-equalizing control which prevents scalding blasts in the shower when toilets are flushed elsewhere on the supply line. Tub spout at right has built-in shower diverter fitting.

Rite-Temp control by Kohler does away with sudden bursts of hot and cold water caused by fluctuations in the available water supply. The unit comes in four finishes.

Speakman's Anystream shower head provides invigorating needle-to-full flood water distribution throughout flow circle.

Moen's deluxe shower head assures full section of water pattern from needle spray to large droplets. A large ball joint permits easy swivel of the head to direct the stream where desired. Construction includes solid brass and Delrin plastic.

Harcraft's Crystal Glo shower head fits any standard 1/2 pipe shower outlet and has finger-tip volume control.

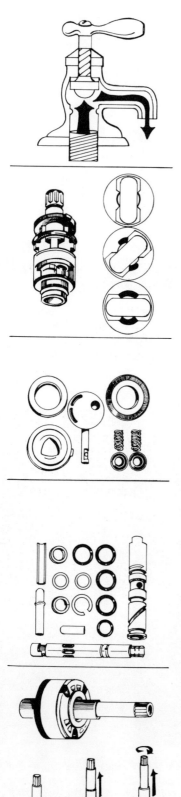

Standard Compression Valve (1)

As illustrated on this page, two-handle faucet sets operate with threaded stems controlled by the handles. The stems screw out to open the supply port and screw in to seal the supply ports. Known as a compression valve, this type faucet has been around for nearly a hundred years.

Disc-to-Disc Type (2)

A newer, two-handle type of faucet uses disc-to-disc contact and has no threads. The lower disc is movable, controlled by a standard handle, and the other disc has ports that are exposed as the cover disc is turned. The more you turn the handle, the more the port is opened and the greater the flow of water. Full-off to full-on is accomplished by only a quarter-turn of the handle. This type faucet has no threads, washers, or packing and the o-ring is not exposed to friction or wear.

Ball-and-Socket Units (3)

Single-handle-control faucets, which have grown greatly in popularity over the past decade, include a ball-and-socket type that operates something like an automobile stick-shift. The lever is moved up and down to control volume and left or right to control temperature. As the lever is moved, the holes in the ball line up with those in the socket.

Cartridge Type (4)

Another type of single-lever faucet works with a cam that is pulled out to control water flow, and turned right or left for temperature control. The tapered shape of the cam controls the flow of the water by direct sealing of the ports. The interchangeable cartridge has no metal-to-metal friction and is self-adjusting and self-lubricating. If the faucet requires maintenance, the entire cartridge is replaced.

Tapered Cam Mechanism (5)

Still another of the newest types on the market is the single-handle unit with a cam that is pulled out to control water flow. The tapered shape controls water volume by opening and sealing ports. Here again, turning the handle left or right controls temperature. This kind of faucet is easy to operate, is permanently lubricated and its single moving part is completely isolated from water to provide years of maintenance-free usage.

When you purchase a faucet, ask the seller for a written warranty. Quality faucets, like other appliances, have written warranties to back them up.

12 Medicine Cabinets and Accessories

Just as the accessories added to a new automobile create buyer interest, accessories used in the bathroom as finishing touches often become determining factors in whether a bathroom is appealing and comfortable, or dull and haphazard-looking.

While you have a virtually unrestricted choice of bathroom accessories today, you should select items to harmonize with fixtures, color scheme and linens used in the room. Budget, of course, will also be a determining factor.

The basic bathroom accessory "package" includes towel bars, combination soap holder-rail (grab bar) for tub or shower, roll paper holder, tumbler holder, soap holder and robe hook. In addition, you may wish to include a towel ladder or tree, built-in-wall scale, lingerie drying line, combination magazine rack-tissue holder, towel rings, built-in hamper, lavatory-mounted lotion dispenser, safety grab bars, sun and heat lamps, bathtub whirlpool unit, exhaust fan, etc. The basic wall-secured accessories are available in polished brass, brushed brass, chromium, brushed chromium, aluminum, vinyl, antique porcelain, gold-plated brass, and ceramic to match or harmonize with ceramic wall tile. Special heating and warming devices are available to keep the floor snug, prevent mirror fogging, eliminate water tank condensation, and even warm your bath towel.

Another important contributor to bathroom decor is the medicine cabinet. Contemporary medicine cabinets are a far cry from the sterile-appearing unit of a dozen years ago. Many are tastefully framed in richly carved wood while others have sleek anodized aluminum lines. Built-in units can be as large as you wish and have space for toilet articles, with sliding mirrors to completely conceal their presence.

Manufactured medicine cabinets can be recessed in the wall or surface-mounted. The units are offered

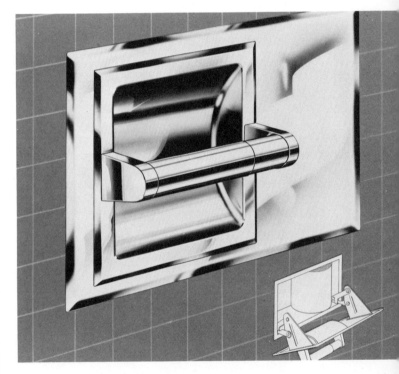

Hall-Mack's two-roll paper holder conceals an extra roll of toilet tissue in compartment behind. The chrome-recessed unit pulls forward for access to the second roll. Fits 10-5/8 × 5-1/3 × 4 inch wall opening.

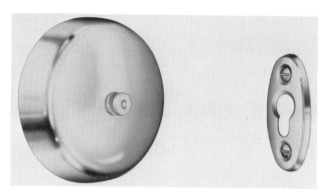

Lingerie line by Hall-Mack provides up to 10 feet of drying space in stall shower or over the bathtub. Pulling the plastic knob (left) reveals spring-tensioned nylon cord that is hooked into retainer plate on opposite wall.

in a wide range of sizes to satisfy practically every decorating need. Most have removable, adjustable shelves and many can merely be turned upside down to reverse the swing of the mirror-door. Still others have mirror doors that tilt for better viewing.

Regardless of the type or number of accessories you select, be sure they are securely attached to prevent accidents and wall damage. Also, be sure to keep radios and portable lamps away from the tub and shower areas, where a person touching one could be electrocuted.

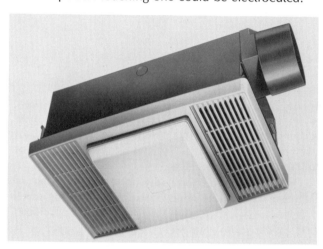

Broan's combination unit takes the chill out of the air when you step from a warm shower, removes mirror fogging and unpleasant odors, and bathes the room with soft light. The ventilator and heater function independently and each function has its own switch. The housing measures 8-1/4 × 14-1/4 × 5-3/4 inches.

Antique gold or white-on-gold oval door of the Grande Duchess by Miami-Carey has a removable mounting pin which permits installation of the cabinet body before mounting the door. The cabinet is recessed and may be used as a right- or left-hand door swing. Glass shelves are removable and adjustable.

The mirror of Miami-Carey's Vista medicine cabinet is framed in walnut with gold-edged linen inner frame. The mirror size is 14 × 22 inches, while the cabinet takes a rough wall opening of the same dimension.

Heat-A-Ventlite three-in-one combination fixtures from NuTone can be round or rectangular in shape. The units come with three on/off controls.

Called the Lady Alsons, this personal mirror swings, tilts and vertically adjusts a full ten inches. Its good-sized nine inch magnifying mirror reflects a large clear image for easy viewing. The chrome bar permits wall mounting. Ideal for makeup or shaving.

111

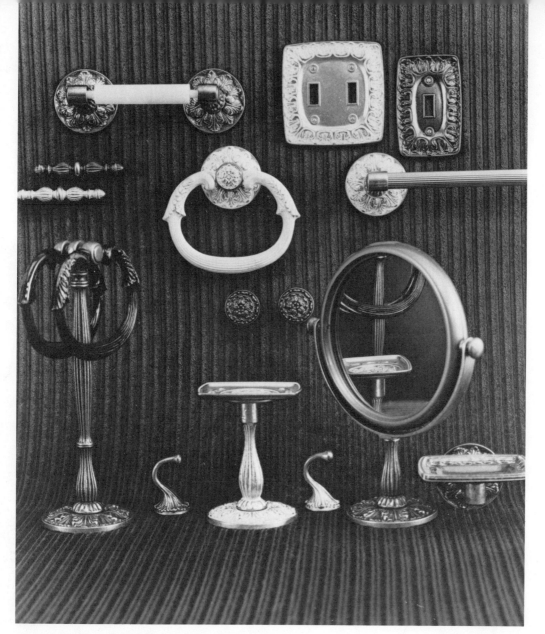

Bath and powder room accessories from Kirsch include
traditional and pewter patterns for shower rods, towel bars
and rings, soap dish-toothbrush holder, vanity mirror, hooks,
switch plates, knobs and pulls, and tumbler holder.

Designed for safe seating in the bath or shower area, this
hand-rubbed natural finish teak wood seat folds against the
wall when not in use. It measures 18-1/2 × 13-1/2 inches
when in use and is anchored with concealed wall
mountings. The unit is manufactured by Alsons Products
Corp.

Economy vanity ensembles can be surface mounted and incorporate illumination, convenience outlet, mirror, and storage cabinet with visible shelf storage. NuTone.

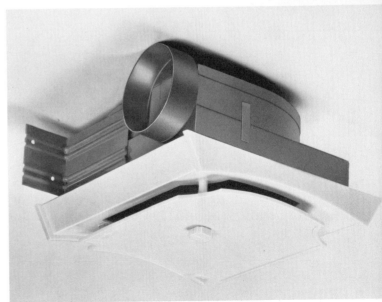

Fasco bathroom ventilators occupy the area of a 12 × 12-inch ceiling tile and feature a plastic design which eliminates rust, mildew, and corrosion. The units provide quiet removal of stale air and moisture, may be painted or papered to match the room decor, and are designed for fast connection to a 3-inch duct.

TriVista and Mini TriVista decorator bath cabinets from NuTone may be recessed or surface mounted in bath and powder rooms. The larger model comes in a choice of 38- or 50-inch mirror widths, while the Mini model has an overall mirror size of 34 × 26 inches.

Twirl-a-Mirror surface mounted medicine cabinets by General Bathroom feature a center door which opens to reveal a magnified mirror for personal grooming. The cabinets are available in 36, 48, and 60-inch widths.

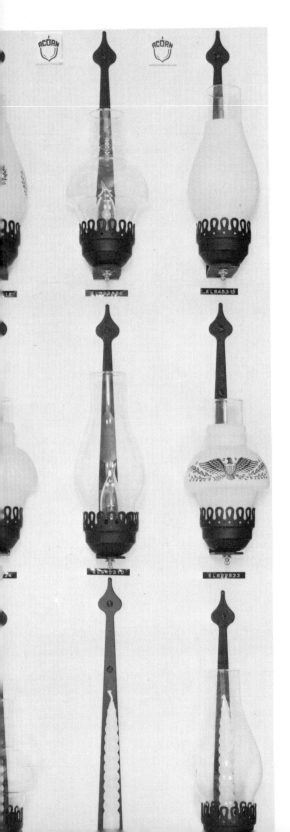

Wrought iron bath accessories from Acorn Manufacturing Co. are augmented by a companion line of chimney-globe light fixtures and candle holders. Square-head screws are used to secure all to the wall.

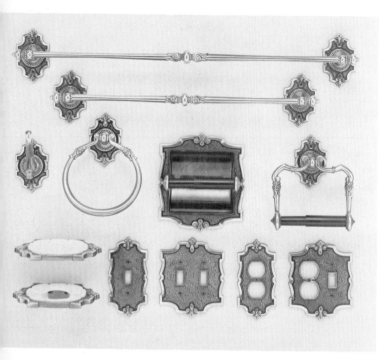

Accessories, while always functional, can also add a touch of elegance to a new or remodeled bathroom. Antique brass items from Ajax Hardware's Premiere Collection have been used for this setting.

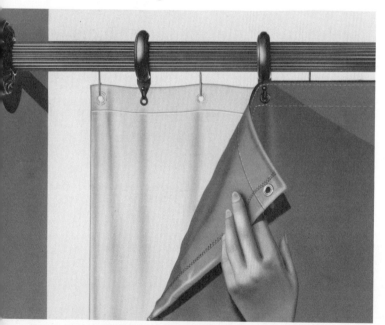

A dual-track shower rod has been introduced to meet the growing trend to use separate lines under handsome fabric shower curtains. Sliding carriers in the back of the rod handle the liner. Separate decorative rings ride in a second track and hold either grommered shower curtains or pinch pleated fabric draperies. Kirsch Co.

This new three-bulb radiant ceiling heater provides instant heat at the flick of a switch. The NuTone unit is prewired for individual control of one or all three lamps together. The anodized aluminum ceiling plate has a 16-inch diameter.

General Bathroom's Tilt-A-Mirror bathroom cabinet is available with either gold or silver anodized aluminum framing in 36-, 48- and 60-inch widths. This surface-mounted cabinet provides three-way viewing plus a center mirror that tilts to offer a full-length view. Theatrical lighting is optional.

NuTone offers quiet exhaust fans for both wall and ceiling installations in bathrooms and powder rooms. The wall unit (left) has a two-piece grille and concealed air-intake ports. Center panel may be decorated to match bath decor or used as accent. The ceiling unit is designed with a pebble-grained grille fitting almost flush with the ceiling.

13 Maintenance and Repair

The old adage, "an ounce of prevention is worth a pound of cure" could well have been written with only the bathroom in mind. For it is here that periodic inspection and a little elbow grease can eliminate the need for future major repairs. Water vapor, leaky faucets and tanks, clogged drains, and loose surfacing materials are the main items to watch for in bathroom maintenance.

Water Vapor

The presence of excess moisture in a bathroom can lead to many costly problems. As explained earlier in this book, vapor-resistant materials should be used and proper ventilation included in all new and remodeled bathrooms. An average shower bath adds between 1/4 and 1/2 pound of water vapor to the moisture content of a home. Tub baths produce less water vapor, but in both instances a little extra effort can prevent harmful damage. The correct procedure to prevent water vapor from spreading throughout the air in the house while bathing is to open the window a few inches at both the top and bottom, or better yet, turn on the ventilating fan.

Periodic inspection of joints around shower pans, bathtubs and lavatories will indicate when it is time to recaulk the joints to prevent water from seeping into the framing members and causing rot. Easy-to-use caulking can be purchased in self-dispensing containers at hardware stores and lumber dealers. In homes with crawl-space foundations, it is well to check under the floor once or twice a year for possible leaks.

Walls, Floors, Ceilings

Painted surfaces in a bathroom can be maintained with a sponge or cloth and soap, detergent or liquid cleaners. Be careful to determine that paint on your walls is washable and always follow the instructions given with the cleanser you purchase.

When it comes time to repaint your bathroom, make sure that the paint you buy will be compatible with that on the walls originally. Save the label off the new paint can so you can be sure to obtain a compatible paint when it again comes time to repaint. Chemical differences in various types of paint mean that some will not bond together properly. If paint peels off the wall or ceiling, remove all loose areas before applying the new coating.

Walls covered with washable wallpaper or vinyl wall covering are kept clean with a damp sponge. Should your bathroom be decorated with unwashable wallpaper, use standard wallpaper cleaner. Test the cleaner in a corner to make certain it will not remove the color or pattern. If it does, the wall cannot be cleaned beyond dusting with a dry cloth and you may wish to repaper the room with washable material.

Walls surfaced with ceramic, metal or plastic tile can be quickly cleaned with a sponge or soft cloth and soap-free detergent (like Fantastik) or washing soda. After rinsing with clear water, an old bath towel can be used to dry the surface. If hard water scale is present, a mild acid cleaner such as Tile-Glow may be used for crystalline glazes and Hillyard's CSP may be used for all other tiles. If quarry tile is used for the wall or floor surface, it may be kept clean by washing with a neutral detergent such as Hillyard's Super Shine-All. Some quarry tiles, particularly imported varieties, are porous and require a penetrating sealer or finish to protect the surface.

Grout, the material used to fill the joints between the tile, comes in a variety of types including silicone rubber, polyurethane (only in factory-grouted sheets), epoxy, acid-resistant, ceramic mosaic, mastic, and sand and cement. The newer silicone materials are highly stain-resistant, mildew-proof, waterproof and noncrack-ing. Soiled grout joints between tiles can be cleaned with a small fiber brush and scouring powder or house-hold bleach. More difficult stains may require a grout cleaner. Harsh abrasives should not be used on glazed tile, nor should ceramic tile be waxed.

Cracked ceramic tile is best repaired by replacing with a new tile. Carefully break the damaged tile with a hammer and stone chisel, clean the mortar surface, spread the back of the new tile with mortar, and set it firmly in place. Permit the tile to dry for a day and then use a wet sponge to thoroughly saturate the tile edges. Grout is then applied in a consistency of thick cream. Use a sponge to wipe off any residue from the tile face while it is still wet.

Cracks or scars in plaster or gypsum wallboard can be repaired with spackling putty available from hardware stores. Patching plaster is used for larger sections of damaged plaster walls, while damaged areas of gypsum wallboard are cut out and replaced with new material. Tape-joint material for this repair can also be purchased at hardware and lumber stores.

Linoleum countertops, floors and backsplashes can be cleaned with soap and water. An occasional buffing with a good paste or liquid wax protects the material and polishes the surface. Use of an electric polisher for the floor heightens the polish and lessens the effort required. To repair linoleum that has become loose carefully roll the material back to the point where it is securely fastened, and remove the old paste from the underside. Check to see that the felt underlayment is securely in place and check also for signs of water leakage, which loosens linoleum. Repaste the linoleum and press it back into position.

Laminated plastic surfaces in the bathroom are easily cleaned with a cloth or sponge and soap and water. Should a sheet of this covering work loose, remove it and, after cleaning the undersurface, apply contact cement to both the underside of the panel and the wall or counter base. Permit both areas to dry and then join them once again, applying pressure with a roller or rubber mallet. Cut a piece of paper slightly larger than the panel to be applied. Place this paper between the panel and surface and after positioning the panel, slowly remove the paper by pulling from one end. Contact bond adhesive sets rapidly when the two coated sheets meet and thus cannot be repositioned. Scratched surfaces can be repaired with matching-color crayons and a coat of wax.

Plumbing Fixtures

Plumbing fixtures are made for, and will have, a long life when given reasonable care. In remodeling, redecorating or making bathroom repairs, never walk on fixtures with shoes. If you are working or painting around fixtures, cover them with old blankets or padding to prevent any chipping. Take care also not to drop bottles, tools, etc., which could chip surfaces.

Hair dyes, spilled cosmetics, leaky faucets and bath mats frequently cause plumbing fixture stains which can usually be removed with a cleanser that will not harm the porcelain enamel or baked enamel surface. Such cleansers are in common supply at supermarkets. Stubborn stains usually can be removed by soaking the area with a weak solution of household bleach or a solution of oxalic acid in water. Manufacturers caution against the use of strong cleansing powders which cause surface wear and lead to stained areas. Harsh abrasives, steel wool and drain-cleaning chemicals also can harm the surface of your fixtures.

Chipped enamel on the edge of a lavatory, bathtub or water closet can be repaired with a liquid porcelain glaze patching compound. More extensive repairs of chipped enamel in bathtubs and lavatories can be handled by professional firms usually listed in the telephone yellow pages under "bathtub repair." Cracked water closets cannot be repaired and should be replaced.

Mechanical bowl stoppers on occasion will not close tightly or open as fully as desired. This problem can be eliminated by adjusting the rod "eye" fastened to the pull rod which runs from the stop of the faucet fitting to beneath the lavatory bowl.

Fiberglass plumbing fixtures, while stain and acid resistant, require reasonable care. These units should be wiped with a damp cloth or use soap and water or a mild dishwashing detergent. Never use scouring powders or pads. Minor stains and cigarette burns in fiberglass may be removed by rubbing lightly with scouring powder and 600 grit sandpaper. Repolish the area with automotive wax. Burning cigarettes should not come in contact with the surface of fiberglass fixtures.

Water Damage and Repairs

Other common bathroom problems can be attribut-ed to one element—water. Most homeowners are famil-iar with leaky faucets and have at one time or another had experience with a water closet tank that refused to stop running. These problems are usually easily solved.

Lavatory, tub, or shower faucet washers are replaced by first removing the cap nut directly under the handle and using the handle to unscrew the stem from the faucet. At the bottom of the stem you will find a washer held in place with a brass screw. Frequently both screw and washer will need replacing to eliminate the leak. Stem grease, which is tasteless and odorless, can be purchased at plumbing repair shops for less than a dollar and easily applied to stem threads to make the stem open and close more smoothly. Before using the grease, lightly sand the stem to remove any corrosion.

Water seepage around the faucet handle is usually caused by worn-out packing under the cap nut. Use an ice pick to remove the old material and replace it with grease-impregnated packing from the hardware store.

Newer single-handle lavatory and shower controls use a cartridge mechanism for control of water, temperature, and polarity. This entire cartridge is replaceable in the event of water leakage.

In replacing washers or cartridges, first turn off the water supply before repairing. Be sure to cover wrench teeth with adhesive tape or use material between the wrench and fixture to prevent scratching. Don't force any parts that do not come apart easily.

Clogged drains in bathrooms are most frequently caused by pieces of soap, hair and lint. If your drains become stopped up with annoying frequency, it may be that improper original installation, wrongly sized pipes, corrosion on inside of pipes, or clogged vent pipes, may be causing your difficulty. A plumber should be called.

Lavatory bowls are equipped with traps that can be drained by removing a screw plug at the bottom curve. Frequently doing so will eliminate the blockage or clogged condition. If not, a "plumbers friend" or toilet plunger can be used to clean the stoppage. To use this device, partially fill the bowl with water, place the cup of the plunger over the drain opening and work the handle up and down several times. This causes alternating compression and suction sufficient to clear many stoppages. A stiff wire forced into the drain opening often works when the plunger fails. Likewise, a chemical drain cleaner may also be used, but the directions should be carefully followed and care should be given to not spilling the solution on surrounding surfaces.

Toilet tank leaks, squeaks, and whistles can be attributed to one or both of two problems—the water supply does not shut off or the outlet valve does not close. Mechanisms within the water tanks vary according

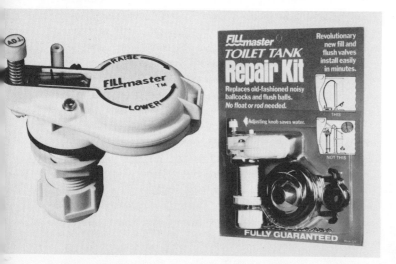

The Fillmaster toilet tank fill valve replaces noisy, leaky ballcocks and eliminates the need for float or rod. Installed easily in minutes, the Fillmaster has a built-in filter screen to prevent valve clogging and fits all tanks. The unit has a simple adjusting knob on top to control the height of the water in the tank and saves up to one gallon per flush.

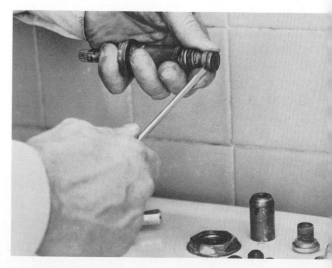

Leaky faucets can be costly as well as causing fixture stains. Replacement of a washer will usually eliminate the problem. Note how the old washer at the end of the stem has been flattened. New washers are in the foreground.

to brand but are designed to produce enough water for thorough flushing of the bowl and then to replace this supply within a minute or so. The accompanying sketch of the most common mechanism found within a water closet tank indicates what should happen when you push the handle to flush the toilet. The rod attached to the handle lifts the tank ball, opens the outlet, and permits water to flow into the toilet bowl. The tank ball then falls back into place, closing the outlet and the tank is refilled from the inlet tube. As the water refills the tank, it raises the float ball which measures the water and closes the supply valve at the proper level.

When water continues to run into the closet bowl after the toilet is flushed, some part of the mechanism in the flush tank is out of order and needs adjustment or replacement. Leaks are usually caused by improper seating of the tank ball. Check to see that the ball wire and rod guide are not bent. Another possible cause of the water failing to shut off when the tank is full is a worn washer in the intake valve. To replace this washer you may have to remove a lever, but shut off the water supply to the tank before doing so. A badly corroded tank mechanism should be replaced.

The "plumber's helper" may be the first step in solving the problem of a clogged toilet. However, instead of the bulb-type suction-cup style unit used for lavatories, you will need a molded-force-ball type which exerts a great deal more pressure.

Leave several inches of water in the toilet bowl and insert the plunger into the opening and start pumping. If the plunger doesn't do the job, you may need a closet auger to break loose the obstruction. If this doesn't work, chances are the toilet will have to be removed from the floor—and it's time to call a plumber.

Preparing for Winter Absences

When closing your home for a vacation or longer period of time, care should be given to protecting the plumbing fixtures. This is especially necessary in cold climates if the house heating system will not be operating.

Begin by turning off the main water supply valve and opening all interior and exterior faucets and pipe drains. All sink and lavatory traps should also be drained and the toilet bowl emptied. The water heater should be turned off and drained. Some type of anti-freeze should then be put into the toilet bowl to keep it from cracking. Kerosene is often used for this purpose.

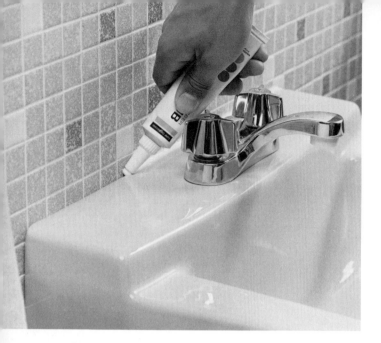
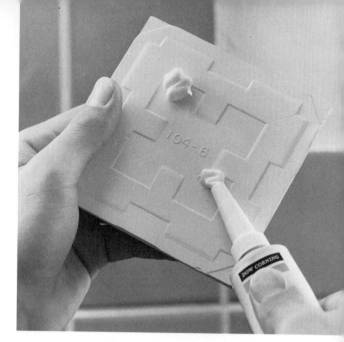

Silicone rubber bathtub caulk can be used to readhere complete ceramic tiles or tile chips as well as to seal tubs, lavatory bowls, and faucets. The material comes in white and decorator pastels, in handy application tubes. Dow Corning photos.

How to Repair a Toilet

Leaky flush valves attributable to conventional toilet tank mechanism can be quickly eliminated with a Flusher Fixer Kit available from hardware and lumber dealers. The kit replaces the worn-out tank ball or flapper and does away with lift wires and brackets that often become bent. Unlike conventional flush valve assemblies, the Flusher Fixer Kit is installed without tools and without removing the tank from the bowl. The kit's seat is simply bonded directly onto the existing seat with a patented watertight sealant.

As detailed in the accompanying photographs, the old tank stopper ball is first removed from the toilet along with the left wires and bracket guide (Illustration 1). Steel wool is then used to clean off the old brass flush valve seat and water used to rinse the seat clean (Illustration 2). Waterproof sealant is applied to the underside of the new stainless steel seat ring using the entire contents of the tube supplied with the kit (Illustration 3).

After placement of the new seat on the old brass seat, a 9-ounce can is placed atop the unit to apply necessary bonding weight. The seat is allowed to set in this position for two hours with water level just enough to cover the top rim of the seat (Illustration 4). A chain is then secured to the flush valve and attached to the lift arm. Excess chain may be cut off or fastened to the clip and the toilet is ready for use (Illustration 5).

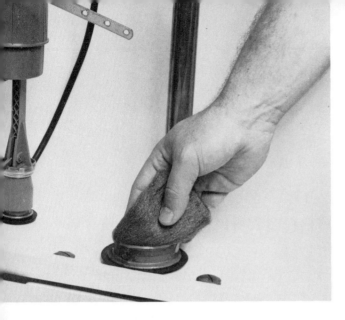
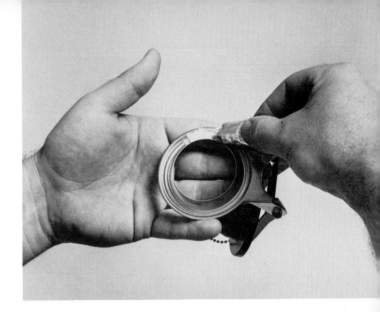
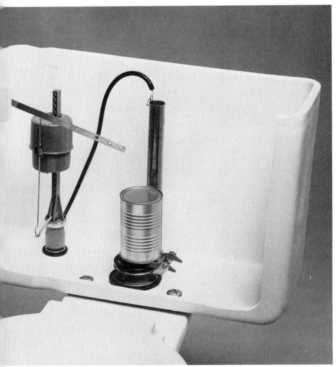
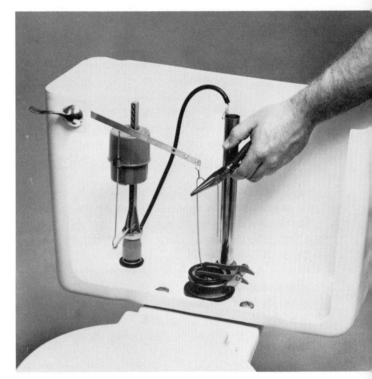
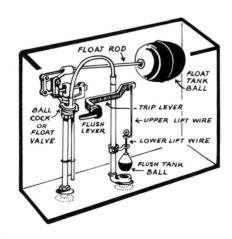

FLOAT ROD

FLOAT TANK BALL

BALL COCK OR FLOAT VALVE

FLUSH LEVER

TRIP LEVER

UPPER LIFT WIRE

LOWER LIFT WIRE

FLUSH TANK BALL

14 Safety in the Bathroom

The bathroom is such a familiar area of the house that we all tend to forget it can also be one of the most dangerous. Here, within a relatively small space, the hazards of water and electricity can combine to cause injury and even death.

Consumer activist Ralph Nader reports that nearly 900 Americans die every year as a result of injuries suffered in bathrooms, and another 187,000 are hurt seriously enough to require hospitalization or emergency room treatment. Falls, burns, cuts, electrocutions—all are possible.

The National Safety Council warns that "tile floors are a real threat when wet. Keep them wiped dry and use a non-skid mat on the floor, especially near the tub or shower where there is likely to be water on the floor."

Most fatal falls in the home admittedly involve the elderly and for this reason special attention should be given to bathroom planning for safety for this group (see Chapter 1). But although the elderly suffer the most severe injuries, not a single age group escapes the threat of accident.

Manufacturers are now producing bathtubs with permanent no-slip surfaces, but bathroom fixtures last for many years so that millions of homes have only the old type of tub with slippery porcelain enamel underfoot. Some type of non-skid mat or surface should be provided, along with sturdy grab bars.

Burns can occur in a bathroom probably more frequently than in any other room of a home, except around the kitchen range. The hazards of gushing hot water to infants and small children are notorious as a cause of death and disfigurement. But even adults can suffer, especially where a too-narrow shower pipe can cause a sudden rush of hot water when cold water is turned on elsewhere in the house. There are simple means to avoid this hazard. The National Safety Council

recommends mixer faucets on the washbowl and a mixer valve or faucet in the shower. The most practical immediate step is simply to make sure the thermostat on the hot water heater is kept at a safe level. Water heated to 115° Fahrenheit or above is destructive to human tissue.

Electricity in combination with the water sources in a bathroom probably is the greatest hazard of all. Lighting fixtures, electrical outlets, and wall switches, all are grouped around washbowls, water closets, tubs, and showers. Human beings using this room frequently have damp hands, damp bodies, or are standing on damp floors. Any malfunction in an electrical appliance can be disastrous.

The danger of shock could be completely eliminated by installation of a ground fault circuit interrupter at the fuse box of the house. These are now required in most building codes for outdoor electrical receptacles, and would be a great factor in improving home safety if they were considered equally important inside a house.

Some of the other common bathroom hazards are pinpointed in this simple home safety quiz for the bathroom provided by the National Safety Council:

Do you:
1. Have non-skid mats or textured surfaces in tubs and showers?
2. Have a sturdy grab bar for your tub or shower?
3. Have medicines clearly labeled and read the label before taking any medicine?
4. Keep medicines stored safely out of the reach of small children?
5. Dry your hands before using electrical appliances—and *never* operate them when you're in the bathtub?
6. Avoid using hair sprays near open flame or when smoking?

Manufacturers List

Ajax Hardware Corporation
825 S. Ajax Ave.
City of Industry, Ca. 91749

Alsons Corp.
Somerset, Mi. 49281

American Olean Tile Co.
Lansdale, Pa. 19446

Am-Finn Sauna
Div. of Urethane Fabricators, Inc.
Haddon Ave. and Line St.
Camden, N.J. 08103

American-Standard
Box 2003
New Brunswick, N.J. 08903

Armstrong Cork Co.
Lancaster, Pa. 17604

Barclay Industries, Inc.
65 Industrial Rd.
Lodi, N.J. 07644

Borg-Warner Corp.
Plumbing Products Div.
Mansfield, Oh.

Bradley Corp.
Menomonee, Wi. 53051

Briggs
5200 W. Kennedy Blvd.
Tampa, Fla. 33609

Broan Manufacturing Co., Inc.
Box 140
Hartford, Wi. 53027

Chicago Specialty Manufacturing
 Co.
7500 Linder Ave.
Skokie, Ill. 60076

Connor Forest Industries
Wausau, Wi. 54401

Crane Co.
300 Park Ave.
N.Y., N.Y.

Dow Corning Corp.
Midland, Mi. 48640

DuPont
Wilmington, Del. 19898

Eljer Plumbing Div.
3 Gateway Center
Pittsburgh, Pa. 15222

Evans Products Co.
1121 S. W. Salmon St.
Portland, Ore, 97208

Fasco Industries, Inc.
Fayetteville, N.C. 28302

Fiat
Div. of Formica Corp.
Cincinnati, Oh. 45202

Fluidmaster, Inc.
1800 Via Burton
Box 4264
Anaheim, Ca. 92803

Formco, Inc.
7745 School Rd.
Cincinnati, Oh. 45242

Formica Corp.
Formica Bldg.
120 E. 4th St.
Cincinnati, Oh. 45202

General Bathroom Products Corp.
2201 Touhy Ave.
Elk Grove Village, Ill. 60007

Gerber Plumbing Fixtures
4656 W. Touhy Ave.
Chicago, Ill. 60648

Haas Cabinet Co., Inc.
Sellersburg, Ind. 47172

Harcraft, Inc.
19110 S. Western Ave.
Torrance, Ca. 90509

Hoover Bathroom Accessories
Fowlerville, Mi. 48836

Jacuzzi Research Inc.
1440 San Pablo Ave.
Berkeley, Ca. 94702

Kirsch Co.
Sturgis, Mi. 49091

Kohler Co.
Kohler, Wi. 53044

Long-Bell Div.
International Paper Co.
Longview, Wa. 98632

Mansfield Sanitary, Inc.
150 First St.
Perrysville, Oh. 44864

Marlite Div.
Masonite Corp.
Dover, Oh. 44622

Masonite Corp.
29 N. Wacker Dr.
Chicago, Ill. 60606

Miami-Carey
203 Garver Rd.
Monroe, Oh. 45050

Milwaukee Faucets, Inc.
4250 N. 124th St.
Milwaukee, Wi. 53222

Moen Faucet
377 Woodland Ave.
Elyria, Oh. 44035

NuTone Div.
Scovill Manufacturing
Madison & Redbank Rds.
Cincinnati, Oh. 45227

Owens-Corning Fiberglas
Fiberglas Tower
Toledo, Oh. 43659

Peerless Faucet Co.
Box 31
Greensburg, Ind. 47240

Powers Regulator Co.
3400 Oakton St.
Skokie, Ill. 60076

Rain Jet Corp.
301 S. Flower St.
Burbank, Ca. 91503

Sherle Wagner International, Inc
60 E. 57th St.
N.Y., N.Y. 10022

Shower Shield
3293 E. 11th Ave.
Hialeah, Fl. 33013

Speakman Co.
Wilmington, Del. 19899

Swan Corp.
721 Olive St.
St. Louis, Mo. 63101

Tile Council of America
Box 326
Princeton, N.J. 08540

Thermasol
101 Park Ave.
N.Y., N.Y. 10017

Triangle Pacific Cabinet Corp.
4255 LBJ Freeway
Dallas, Tex. 75234

Tub-Master Corp.
413 Virginia Dr.
Orlando, Fla. 32803

Universal-Rundle Corp.
Box 960
New Castle, Pa. 16103

Viking Sauna Co.
909 Park Ave.
San Jose, Ca. 95150

Wasco Products, Inc.
Box 351
Sanford, Me. 04073

Wilson Plastics Co.
600 General Bruce Dr.
Temple, Tex. 76501

Window Shade Manufacturers
 Assn.
230 Park Ave.
N.Y., N.Y. 10017

Z-Brick Co.
2834 N.W. Market St.
Seattle, Wa. 98107

Index